Agency Problems
and
Financial Contracting

Amir Barnea
Faculty of Management
Tel Aviv University

Robert A. Haugen
Graduate School of Business
University of Wisconsin-Madison

Lemma W. Senbet
Graduate School of Business
University of Wisconsin-Madison

Prentice-Hall, Inc., Englewood Cliffs, New Jersey 07632

Library of Congress Cataloging in Publication Data

Barnea, Amir.
  Agency problems and financial contracting.

  (Prentice-Hall foundations of finance series)
  Bibliography: p. 144
  Includes index.
  1. Corporations—Finance.   2. Agency (Law)
I. Haugen, Robert A.   II. Senbet, Lemma W.   III. Title.
IV. Title: Financial contracting.   V. Series.
HG4011.B355 1985   658.1'5   84-17702
ISBN 0-13-018854-9
ISBN 0-13-018847-6 (pbk.)

Editorial/production supervision: Pam Price
Manufacturing buyer: Ed O'Dougherty

Printed in the United States of America

10 9 8 7 6 5 4 3 2 1

ISBN 0-13-018854-9   01

ISBN 0-13-018847-6   [Pbk]

Prentice-Hall International, Inc., *London*
Prentice-Hall of Australia Pty. Limited, *Sydney*
Editora Prentice-Hall do Brasil, Ltda., *Rio de Janeiro*
Prentice-Hall Canada Inc., *Toronto*
Prentice-Hall of India Private Limited, *New Delhi*
Prentice-Hall of Japan, Inc., *Tokyo*
Prentice-Hall of Southeast Asia Pte. Ltd., *Singapore*
Whitehall Books Limited, *Wellington, New Zealand*

PRENTICE-HALL FOUNDATIONS OF FINANCE SERIES

Amir Barnea, Robert A. Haugen, and Lemma W. Senbet
Agency Problems and Financial Contracting

Harold Bierman, Jr.
The Lease Versus Buy Decision

Herbert E. Dougal and Jack E. Gaumnitz
Capital Markets and Institutions, 4th Edition

Gunter Dufey and Ian H. Giddy
The International Money Market

Jack Clark Francis and Stephen H. Archer
Portfolio Analysis, 2nd Edition

George H. Hempel and Jess B. Yawitz
Financial Management of Financial Institutions

David A. Ricks
International Dimensions of Corporate Finance

James C. Van Horne
Function and Analysis of Capital Market Rates

PRENTICE-HALL FOUNDATIONS OF FINANCE SERIES

Ezra Solomon, *Editor*

Contents

Editor's Note

The subject matter of financial management is in the process of rapid change. A growing analytical content, virtually nonexistent ten years ago, has displaced the earlier descriptive treatment as the center of emphasis in the field.

These developments have created problems for both teachers and students. On the one hand, recent and current thinking, which is addressed to basic questions that cut across traditional divisions of the subject matter, do not fit neatly into the older structure of academic courses and texts in corporate finance. On the other hand, the new developments have not yet stabilized and as a result have not yet reached the degree of certainty, lucidity, and freedom from controversy that would permit all of them to be captured within a single, straightforward treatment at the textbook level. Indeed, given the present rate of change, it will be years before such a development can be expected.

One solution to the problem, which the present Foundations of Finance Series tries to provide, is to cover the major components of the subject through short independent studies. These individual essays provide a vehicle through which the writer can concentrate on a single sequence of ideas and thus communicate some of the excitement of current thinking and controversy. For the teacher and student, the separate self-contained books provide a flexible up-to-date survey of current thinking on each subarea covered and at the same time permit maximum flexibility in course and curriculum design.

EZRA SOLOMON

Preface

Conflicting interests among parties to the corporate firm may lead to suboptimal allocation of resources within the organization. This productive inefficiency manifests itself in the form of "agency problems." The term derives its name from the fact that corporate decisions are delegated to agents (e.g., management) who perform on behalf of other parties (external financiers). Recently agency problems have received rapidly growing attention in finance.

Agency problems in finance can be greatly reduced by efficient operation of the financial and labor markets. The unresolved agency problems can be further mitigated by complex financial contracting, which aligns the diverse and conflicting interests of the parties. This is particularly important in finance, because the process of resolving the agency problems gives rise to complex financial instruments, such as callable and convertible securities. The traditional literature is quite inadequate in explaining the existence of complex and realistic financial contracts that are readily observed in the financial world.

Residual agency problems, which remain unresolved either in the market place or through financial contracting, manifest themselves in the form of reduction in the value of financial securities. Thus, they constitute countervailing costs against the benefits of external financing. This trade-off leads to the existence of optimal financial structure. In the process of generating optimal financial structures for firms, the trade-off gives rise to a yield differential across securities of different status with respect to their propensity to resolve agency problems. Also in this process we obtain insights into who bears agency costs.

Thus, the study of the role of agency problems enriches finance by making it more realistic. In our view to date, no other stronger economic rationale exists to explain corporate financial structure and its associated complexities. This important issue is the subject of this book. The book analytically synthesizes recent published and unpublished works in the area, but it also draws important implications from these studies for corporate financial management, complex financial contracting, the behavior of relative prices of securities, regulation of the securities market, accounting disclosure rules, and the functioning of the financial and labor markets in general. These are issues that go to the heart of finance. The book is intended to communicate these concepts in a concise and readable form to parties who make financial decisions at the corporate level, to individual and organized investors, to students of finance and economics, and to security exchange and accounting regulators.

The book is intended to be used as a supplement for courses in corporate finance, money and capital markets, and financial intermediation, both at the advanced undergraduate and graduate levels. At this time there exists no such treatment of the subject matter in other books or monographs. Although the subject matter is treated with depth and rigor, the mathematical background required in order to understand the material in this book is minimal. It is advisable to have a background in introductory finance and a working knowledge of basic economics. This book covers a timely topic which, we believe, will have a significant impact on finance. We attempt to bring the subject matter to a general level of comprehension without sacrifice in analytical content. Last but not least, the book is intended to stimulate research in the area which, we expect, will be a topic of interest and excitement for the next decade or so.

In the course of preparing the book, we have benefited from colleagues and associates at various universities. In particular, we wish to acknowledge Richard Green (Carnegie Mellon University), Frank Jen (SUNY-Buffalo), Dennis Logue (Dartmouth College), Gershon Mandelker (University of Pittsburgh), and Robert Taggart (Boston University). Anonymous reviewers of the draft gave us suggestions and comments that significantly improved the final product. Our students at the University of Wisconsin–Madison, too many to mention individually, reacted in a very valuable fashion in the course of learning the material as a supplement to relevant textbook chapters in corporate finance. Their reactions were incorporated in the exposition of the book.

We owe special thanks to two editors at Prentice-Hall, David Hildebrand and Linda Frascino; production editor, Pam Price; and the expert staff at Prentice-Hall for handling the review, editorial, and production processes in an extremely professional manner. Of course, we look forward to working with them again in the future on other projects.

Kathy McCord, a word processing expert at Wisconsin, was immensely patient and proficient in producing numerous drafts of the book. We thank her deeply.

```
1111111111111111111111111111111111111111111111111111111111111111111111111111111111
1111111111111111111111111111111111111111111111111111111111111111111111111111111111
111111111111111111111111111111111111111    1111111111111111111111111111111111111111
1111111111111111111111111111111111111111   1111111111111111111111111111111111111111
1111111111111111111111111111111111111111   1111111111111111111111111111111111111111
1111111111111111111111111111111111111111   1111111111111111111111111111111111111111
1111111111111111111111111111111111111111   1111111111111111111111111111111111111111
1111111111111111111111111111111111111111   1111111111111111111111111111111111111111
1111111111111111111111111111111111111111   1111111111111111111111111111111111111111
1111111111111111111111111111111111111111   1111111111111111111111111111111111111111
1111111111111111111111111111111111111111   1111111111111111111111111111111111111111
1111111111111111111111111111111111111111   1111111111111111111111111111111111111111
1111111111111111111111111111111111111111111111111111111111111111111111111111111111
1111111111111111111111111111111111111111111111111111111111111111111111111111111111
```

Introduction

1.1 The Role of Agency Problems

OBSERVED contractual arrangements in finance are complex. A perusal of financial statements issued by U.S. corporations reveals a striking complexity in their capital structure. This ranges from option-type characteristics in preferred stock and debt instruments, such as conversion privileges and call provisions, to maturity structure and repayment arrangements entailing sinking fund provisions. Indeed, it is not uncommon to find debt instruments carrying both conversion and call options simultaneously. The bulk of the tradition in finance focuses only on simple debt and equity securities. Financial complexities are either assumed away or explained on irrational grounds. This is surprising in view of the landmark contributions of J. B. Williams (1938) and Modigliani and Miller (1958), which are based on rationality and efficient operation of financial markets.

This book introduces agency problems as a powerful explanation for observed complexities in financial contracting and optimal corporate finance. Agency problems arise from conflicting interests among parties to the corporate firm, such as management, capital contributors, employees, customers, suppliers, and the government. Unless these problems are resolved they would lead to suboptimal allocation

1

of resources within the organization. The term "agency" derives from the fact that corporate decisions are delegated to agents (e.g., management) who perform on behalf of other parties (external financiers). The process of resolving agency problems through contractual arrangements leads to an evolution of complex finance. The subject matter of the book traces this process by synthesizing recent published and unpublished works in the area and by drawing important implications for issues that go to the heart of finance, namely corporate financial management, complex financial contracting, relative pricing of securities with differential agency cost and tax exposure, and financial synergy in mergers or spin-offs. Thus, the study of the role of agency problems enriches finance by making it more realistic and exciting.

1.2 Organization

This book makes a logical progression from an environment *without* agency problems to an environment *with* agency problems. The focus is on an environment *with* agency problems, which proceeds logically from the world that permits efficient operation of financial and labor markets to the world with frictions and market impediments. Agency problems in finance can be greatly reduced by efficient operation of markets. The unresolved agency problems can be further mitigated by complex financial contracting that aligns the diverse and conflicting interests of the parties. This is particularly important in finance, because as mentioned earlier, the process of resolving agency problems gives rise to complex financial instruments, such as callable and convertible securities. Residual agency problems, which remain unresolved either in the market place or through financial contracting, manifest themselves in the form of reduction in the value of financial securities. Thus, they give rise to countervailing costs against the benefits of external financing. This trade-off leads to optimal corporate finance characterized by complex capital structure and maturity arrangements.

The anatomy of the book is contained in subsequent chapters. Chapter 2 reviews the theory of corporate finance in the absence of agency problems. Such a review accomplishes two purposes. First, it serves as a reminder that a deeper feeling about financial theory *without* agency problems enhances an understanding of the theory *with* agency problems. Second, it serves as a benchmark for the analyses contained in subsequent chapters. This chapter review starts from the celebrated theorem of Franco Modigliani and Merton Miller (MM, 1958) that capital structure policy of the firm is inconsequential to its market valuation under perfect market conditions. The theorem is a fundamental departure from the traditionalist view advocating a judicious financial "cocktail" so as to enhance firm value. The MM arbitrage argument, however, dispels this view by clearly demonstrating that debt possesses no *inherent* advantage when it is merely used as a mechanism to slice the existing pie (firm) into various claims. The MM theorem is then shown to hold even under more generalized uncertainty.

However, imperfections, such as taxes, may create a positive role for corporate finance. This is more apparent than real, however. Corporate taxation alone corners the firm to exclusive debt financing M+M 1963 due to tax deductibility of interest payments. However, once personal income taxation is brought into the picture, the gain from leverage is a function of the *relative* taxation of corporate income, equity income, and bond income. In this sense, it may be *negative*. The gain from leverage is shown to evaporate altogether with appropriate adjustments of supply of debt in equilibrium under certain conditions specified by Miller (1977). Thus, so long as markets operate efficiently to allow marketability of redundant tax shelters, the tax environment alone may be unable to explain observed financial regularities and complexities.

Chapter 3 examines in detail the potential conflicts of interest that may exist between those who contribute capital to the firm. The chapter also examines how these conflicts may result in costs that are borne by the capital contributors. Although the focus of this book is on the financial theory of agency, Chapter 3 discusses certain important links between developments of agency theory in finance with developments in the economics literature. The following are broad classes of agency problems in finance:

A. *On the Job Perquisite Consumption*—The problem of on-the-job consumption of perquisites by a manager with partial ownership interests in the firm.
B. *Risk Incentive*—The incentive of stockholders to adopt high-risk investment projects in order to expropriate wealth from existing bondholders.
C. *Investment Incentive*—The incentive of stockholders to forgo otherwise profitable investment opportunities so as to again expropriate wealth from existing bondholders.
D. *Bankruptcy Costs*—Costs involved in resolving disputes between capital contributors over their respective rights in the event of bankruptcy.
E. *Informational Asymmetry*—In this case, management, acting in the interests of existing securityholders, attempts to raise additional capital from outsiders. Management possesses inside information, but it cannot reveal it to the market because of a moral hazard problem. (There is a conflict of interest between new and existing securityholders.) If management sells the securities to outsiders at undervalued prices, existing securityholders suffer a loss that can be viewed as an agency cost.

Chapter 4 provides the theory of optimal capital structure resulting from (a) the trade-off between agency costs of debt and equity capital and (b) the trade-off between agency costs and tax subsidy. The op-

timality of capital structure hinges critically on the characteristics of
marginal agency costs as functions of the amount of external financing
raised. Certain classes of agency problems, such as risk shifting, depend on the underlying investment opportunity set available to the
firm, and there is no *a priori* reason to expect a *rising* marginal agency
cost function. This chapter examines plausible conditions for such
rising marginal agency cost functions and the associated optimal capital structure. Due to the logical progression pursued in the book,
Chapter 4 abstracts from possible market mechanisms and the issuance of complex financial securities as possible solutions to agency
problems.

Chapter 5 discusses the role of the financial and labor markets,
respectively, in resolving agency problems. The objective is to describe
the potential means by which these markets resolve the conflicting
interests between those parties associated with the firm. The concluding portion of each section is devoted to a discussion of potential
impediments to the market mechanism that may stand as a barrier to
a natural resolution of agency problems. As we shall see, to the extent
that these barriers are significant, investors cannot fully rely on markets to resolve the conflicts of interest that exist between the various
parties to the firm. Instead, they must rely on complex contracts
relating to both managerial compensation and to the nature of the
claims of outsiders to the firm's income.

Chapter 6 analyzes several examples of complex financial contracts
that play a role in eliminating any agency problems remaining unresolved by the market place. These complex contracts include call
provisions in corporate debt, managerial stock options, convertible
debt, income bonds, indenture provisions, pension plans, and corporate by-laws. Thus, this chapter is explicit about the nature of financial contracts that specify sharing rules among securityholders
with divergent interests. In particular, such contracts are vital in resolving the agency problems of risk shifting, informational asymmetry, excessive managerial perquisite consumption, and forgone growth
opportunities. We find that when these problems exist simultaneously,
they call for the coexistence of various complex features in financial
contracting. That is why a strong economic rationale is provided for
the existence of observed complex capital structures consisting not
only of straight debt and equity capital, but also convertible securities,
callable debt, callable-convertible debt, and executive stock options.
Ample graphic and numerical examples, as well as the appendix to
the chapter, provide explicit solutions and mechanisms illustrating
the coexistence of complex financial contracts.

Financial contracts differ in terms of their ability to resolve agency
problems. Chapter 7 examines how this may result in the emergence
of yield differentials between securities. The analysis is basically an
extension of the Miller (1977) equilibrium discussed in Chapter 2.

The introduction of debt-related agency costs and a limited form of tax arbitrage by individual investors affect the conclusion associated with the Miller equilibrium. The generalized equilibrium is characterized by the following properties: (1) corporate capital structure affects market value; (2) agency costs of debt shared by all firms are shifted to bondholders in the form of lower interest rates; and (3) the observable spread between yields on taxable and nontaxable bonds is explained.

Finally, Chapter 8 provides agency applications to other types of contracts and organizational structures, namely investment banking, insurance, financial synergy, and accounting information. The purpose of this chapter is to emphasize the scope and strength of agency theory in rationalizing observable phenomena that are not explained by existing financial theories. For instance, the institutional aspects of investment banking are illuminated in the context of optimal contracts that evolve in the process of risk sharing between the banker and the issuer. Also, a positive theory of accounting may emerge from agency considerations.

```
22222222222222222222222222222222222222222222222222222222222222222222222222222222222
22222222222222222222222222222222222222222222222222222222222222222222222222222222222
2222222222222222222222222222222222222222    222    222222222222222222222222222222222222
2222222222222222222222222222222222222222    222    222222222222222222222222222222222222
2222222222222222222222222222222222222222    222    222222222222222222222222222222222222
2222222222222222222222222222222222222222    222    222222222222222222222222222222222222
2222222222222222222222222222222222222222    222    222222222222222222222222222222222222
2222222222222222222222222222222222222222    222    222222222222222222222222222222222222
2222222222222222222222222222222222222222    222    222222222222222222222222222222222222
2222222222222222222222222222222222222222    222    222222222222222222222222222222222222
2222222222222222222222222222222222222222    222    222222222222222222222222222222222222
22222222222222222222222222222222222222222222222222222222222222222222222222222222222
22222222222222222222222222222222222222222222222222222222222222222222222222222222222
```

Capital Structure in the
Absence of Agency Problems

2.1 Introduction

WHILE the basic theme of this book is to explain corporate financial structure and its associated complexities in the context of agency problems, we shall begin by reviewing the theory of corporate finance in the absence of these incentive problems. Such a review accomplishes two interrelated purposes. First, it serves as a reminder that a deeper feeling about financial theory *without* agency problems enhances an understanding of the theory *with* agency problems. By analogy, as they say, an understanding of the frictionless surface is useful for an understanding of the physics of motion. Second, it serves as a benchmark for the analyses contained in subsequent chapters.

The following section focuses on the celebrated theorem of Franco Modigliani and Merton Miller (MM, 1958) that capital structure policy of the firm is inconsequential to its market valuation under perfect market conditions. The theorem is a fundamental departure from the traditionalist view advocating judicious financial "cocktail" so as to enhance firm value.[1] Traditionalists postulate a U-shaped curve for the overall cost of capital of the firm due to a seemingly plausible argument that the cost of equity remains constant for a small amount of leverage. Thus, according to this view, the value of the firm is maximized at an *interior* capital structure. The MM arbitrage argument, however, dispels this view by clearly demonstrating that debt possesses no *inherent* advantage when it is merely used as a mechanism to slice the existing pie (firm) into various claims. The MM theorem is shown in the next section (2.23) to hold even under more general conditions.

Section 2.3 examines the effect of taxation on corporate financial policy. First, the effect of corporate taxes is shown to enhance the value of the firm due to government subsidy resulting from tax deductibility of interest payments. However, once personal income taxation is brought into the picture, the gain from leverage is a function of the *relative* taxation of corporate income, equity income, and bond income. In this sense, it may be *negative*. Second, the gain from leverage is shown to evaporate altogether with appropriate adjustments of supply of debt in equilibrium under certain conditions specified by Miller (1977).

2.2 The Modigliani-Miller Arbitrage Theorem of Capital Structure

Arbitrage opportunities exist when the Law of One Price is violated. An arbitrageur purchases an item in one market and immediately sells it in another market for a higher price. The intuition behind the MM theorem is that two firms, which are identical in terms of the assets that they hold, should conform to the law of one price, and hence they should sell at the same *total* price despite *differences* in the liabilities issued to finance the assets. In other words, the basic identity between the two commodities (firms) is unaffected by the way they are sliced through some mechanism (e.g., financial leverage) or by the way the securities are packaged. Of course, the act of slicing or packaging must be undertaken without diseconomies or imperfections, consistent with the MM perfect market assumptions. Indeed, the moral of this arbitrage argument is that capital structure *per se* has no *inherent* advantages or disadvantages in altering the *real* aspects of the firm. It is not the product itself; it is merely the package. In the MM world, you can make capital budgeting decisions without worrying about how to raise money! Investment and financing decisions are completely separable.

---

[1] See Ezra Solomon, *The Theory of Financial Management* (New York: Columbia University Press, 1963), pp. 92–98, for an exposition of the traditionalist view.

2.21 The Homogeneous Risk Class Proof of the MM Theorem[2]

Consider the following assumptions.

a. The capital market is *perfectly competitive* in the sense that
   i. Securities are infinitely divisible
   ii. Information is costless and available to all market agents (investors and firms)
   iii. There are no transaction costs or taxes in the issuance or trading of securities
   iv. All market agents are price takers in the capital market
b. Homemade leverage is a perfect substitute for corporate leverage in the sense that any securities that firms can issue against their probability distribution of returns can also be issued on personal account by investors who happen to own assets with equivalent distributions of returns.
c. Debt financing does not entail default risk.
d. Firms can be classified into homogeneous risk classes in the sense that the cash flows to the capital contributors to any firm in any given class are proportional to (and hence perfectly correlated with) the cash flows of any other firm in the same risk class.

The original proof of MM (1958) has a deficiency, as pointed out by Heins and Sprenkle (see footnote 2). Consequently, we wish to employ the spirit of an alternative proof contained in their reply to Heins and Sprenkle. Consider two firms identical in all respects except for their method of financing. Their operating income is $\tilde{X}_U = \tilde{X}_L = \tilde{X}$, where U and L refer to the unlevered and levered firms, respectively. Note that this postulation satisfies the homogeneous risk class assumption contained in (d).[3] The levered firm raises debt (D) at the riskless rate of interest (r). Suppose that the value of the unlevered firm is V_U and the value of the levered firm is $V_L = D + S_L$, where S_L = the value of equity. An investor can then employ alternative strategies yielding equivalent return streams. Two such strategies are shown in Table 2.1. To prevent arbitrage, equivalent return streams should sell at the same price in equilibrium. Thus, if we invoke the Law of One Price, the investor should pay identical amounts so that

---

[2] The original proof of the theorem is contained in F. Modigliani and M. Miller, "The Cost of Capital, Corporation Finance, and the Theory of Investment," *American Economic Review* (June 1958). The more refined proof is provided in F. Modigliani and M. Miller, "Reply to Heins and Sprenkle," *American Economic Review* (September 1969).

[3] The homogeneous risk class assumption is satisfied by $\tilde{X}_U = \alpha\tilde{X}_L$, implying that if they were *unlevered*, the expected return on the stock of the two firms must be identical to prevent arbitrage. The proof above is for $\alpha = 1$.

$$\alpha S_L = \alpha(V_U - D)$$

Hence,

$$V_U = S_L + D = V_L \qquad (1)$$

TABLE 2.1

	Net Investment	Return Stream
Strategy A [Hold α fraction of the levered firm's stock]	αS_L	$\alpha(\tilde{X}_L - rD)$
Strategy B [Hold α fraction of the unlevered firm's stock and borrow αD on personal account]	$\alpha(V_U - D)$	$\alpha(\tilde{X}_U - rD)$

Therefore, (1) establishes the entity theory of value or the familiar MM theorem that the total value of the firm is independent of its financial leverage.[4] It is entirely determined by its operating return stream (X) and its associated risk.[5]

2.22 The MM Arbitrage Theorem and Its Corollaries

Note that given the MM theorem their Proposition II follows directly. That is, the required rate of return on equity increases linearly with financial leverage. Define the required rates of return (or costs of capital) as

$K_U = \overline{X}_U/V_U$; and K_L

$$= (\overline{X}_L - rD)/S_L \text{ (bars denote expectations)} \qquad (2)$$

But

$$\overline{X}_L = \overline{X}_U = K_U V_U; \text{ and } V_U = V_L = S_L + D$$

Substituting the above in (2) and rearranging, we have the MM Proposition II.

$$K_L = K_U + (K_U - r) \, D/S_L \qquad (3)$$

financial premium

---

[4] The original insight behind the entity theory of value is due to J. B. Williams, *The Theory of Investment Value* (Amsterdam: North-Holland Publishing Co., 1938). The work of MM two decades later is, nonetheless, considered as pathbreaking for its rigorous advancement of the theory under conditions of uncertainty and for its rigorous pursuit of the theory's implications for corporate financial issues, such as cost of capital and capital budgeting. Thus, the MM paper constitutes the most rigorous scientific basis for the modern theory of finance.

[5] The two strategies employed in proving the MM theorem are not unique in the sense that alternative strategies exist that lead to the same result in (1). For instance, α of the unlevered stock *and* α of both levered stock and debt should yield an identical return stream such that $\alpha V_U = \alpha(S_L + D) = \alpha V_L$. However, the proof in the text displays the critical role of borrowing on a personal account under the same terms available to the firm.

This does not mean that the *price per share* that you hold changes when the firm alters its financial leverage. To the contrary, the required rate of return on equity increases linearly to maintain the existing price per share. The firm uses debt to "trade on the equity" and increase expected net income available to stockholders, but the required rate of return increases commensurately, thereby rendering the stock price unchanged. In the MM world, the price per share and the value of the firm are unaffected by the expedient of issuing debt and using the proceeds to retire part of the outstanding stock (i.e., by altering financial leverage).

The price equality can be shown by positing an unlevered firm that wishes to undertake capital structure rearrangement. Initially,

$$V_U = NP_U \qquad (4)$$

where

$$N = \text{number of shares outstanding}$$

$$P_U = \text{the price per share of the unlevered stock}$$

If the firm repurchases M shares at the *post*-capital structure rearrangement price (P_L) by using the proceeds from the issuance of debt, its value is

$$V_L = (N - M)P_L + MP_L \qquad (5)$$

where

$$MP_L = D = \text{the proceeds from the debt issue}$$

$$= \text{the value of the debt}$$

But by the MM theorem, $V_L = V_U$, and hence by equating (4) and (5) we obtain

$$P_L = P_U \qquad (6)$$

Thus, (3) and (6) are consistent, because they both follow from (1), the MM arbitrage theorem. The levered equity is more risky than the unlevered equity and the expression in (3) reflects the financial risk premium as a function of financial leverage, but the price per share, nonetheless, remains the same as shown in (6). Note also that the financial risk premium in (3) has nothing to do with default risk, because we have ruled that out with assumption (c) in section (2.21). As the firm retires equity by substituting riskless debt, it magnifies the extent of *risk sharing* by the remaining stockholders. The financial leverage risk premium in (6) reflects this phenomenon,[6] because equityholders of the levered firm are appropriately compensated for incremental risk sharing. In the following subsection, we shall see that the MM theorem can be generalized into conditions of default risk where debtholders share risk with equityholders.

In closing this subsection, we wish to make some additional remarks about the sense in which the MM theorem is important. Imagine that firms offer two products, namely *real* products (e.g., apples and computers) and *financial* products (e.g., debt and equity securities). The intuition behind the MM theorem is that *financial* products merely serve as mechanisms to allocate real products, and hence their value is completely determined by the real sector. In other words, the value of the firm is entirely determined by its activities in the real sector. This is true even if the firm has monopoly power in the real sector, so long as it has no monopoly power in the financial sector. Admittedly, Modigliani and Miller make assumptions that are unlikely to be observed in the real world.[7] However, the power of the MM theorem is in dispelling the traditional illusion that in an environment where packaging and repackaging financial claims to real assets is costless, identical products sold in different packages can be priced differentially. This insight can be assessed only under a "clean" surface, and the assumptions are intended to do just that. Obviously, *environmental* (not genetic!) factors, distortions, or outright discrimination, such as a government tax subsidy in favor of corporate debt, may create relevance for financial products. Before we embark on such environmental factors, however, we need to look at some generalizations of the MM theorem. These generalizations explore certain redundancies or undue restrictions in the MM assumptions or specification of the environment under which their theorem holds. It turns out that the MM environment is too clean (it is beyond EPA requirements!).

2.23 Subsequent Generalizations of the Modigliani-Miller Arbitrage Theorem

Let us relax some of the assumptions while simultaneously maintaining the MM theorem.

---

[6] This can be seen easily through the familiar capital asset pricing model:

$$K_L = r + \lambda \, cov \, (K_L, K_m) \tag{i}$$

where

$$\lambda = \frac{K_m - r}{\sigma_m^2} = \text{the market price of risk}$$

Rewriting (i) as $K_L = r + \lambda \, cov \left(\dfrac{\overline{X}}{S_L}, K_m \right)$, we see that the term in the parentheses is greater for the levered equity, because $S_L < V_U$.

[7] MM also make an additional assumption that dividend policy is of no consequence to the value of the firm. As it turns out, this assumption is unnecessary, because it follows from the rest of the assumptions. See M. Miller and F. Modigliani, "Dividend Policy, Growth and the Valuation of Shares," *Journal of Business* (October 1961).

2.231 IS THE HOMOGENEOUS RISK CLASS ASSUMPTION NECESSARY?

Given assumptions (a), (b), and (c) in section (2.21), it turns out that assumption (d) about homogeneous risk class is not necessary. In other words, the MM theorem can be established even if there exists *no* two or more firms that are identical in real asset characteristics. The general equilibrium proof is provided by Stiglitz.[8] Here we wish to provide the basic economic intuition behind the proof. Suppose that a portfolio equilibrium exists in the market, given the real and financial decisions of firms in the economy. Stiglitz's proof is general in the sense that he envisions a multiperiod framework with investors facing consumption paths through time. At any rate, he establishes that the opportunities for investors to construct their portfolios are entirely unaffected if a particular firm wishes to perturb the equilibrium by changing its financial policy. Investors can undo any financial policy undertaken by the firm if they make appropriate adjustments in their personal borrowing and lending activities.

Let us take a closer look at the offsetting actions that investors can take. Suppose that a particular firm lowers its debt-to-equity ratio by decreasing the number of bonds outstanding. These bonds are retired by issuing new equity. Individuals can borrow on their personal accounts and offset the firm's actions. The proceeds from borrowing are used to buy newly issued equity. Thus, the initial portfolio opportunity set is restored. In the parlance of the traditional mean-variance framework, for instance, the capital market line remains unchanged by changing firm financial policies. The increase in personal borrowing offsets exactly the decrease in corporate borrowing so that the supply and demand for debt continues to be in balance. Consequently, it is not the homogeneous risk class assumption that is critical to the MM theorem but the ability of investors to compete with firms on an equal footing for lending and borrowing activities.[9] The total value of the firm is entirely governed by its *real* decisions; its *financial* policy is inconsequential.

2.232 DOES BANKRUPTCY MATTER?

Up to this point, the MM theorem has been established under conditions of riskless borrowing and lending activities. One might argue

---

[8] J. Stiglitz, "On the Irrelevance of Corporate Financial Policy," *American Economic Review* (December 1974). See, in particular, Theorem I.

[9] L. Senbet and R. Taggart, in their paper, "Capital Structure Equilibrium Under Market Imperfections and Incompleteness," *Journal of Finance* (March 1984), establish the limited MM theorem even when individuals do not compete equally with firms. That is, capital structure is still indeterminate at the individual firm level but not at the aggregate level. Thus, the crucial assumption, and indeed the *only* assumption, needed for this limited case is costless corporate leverage, which need not be duplicated by personal leverage.

that default risk or bankruptcy may disturb perfect substitutability between personal leverage and homemade leverage. This problem is demonstrated analytically by Baron.[10] The original MM risk class assumption tends to obscure this fact, because even under bankruptcy, firms of the same risk class are shown to have the same *common* value, despite differences in capital structure. However, in a general portfolio equilibrium framework, the common value itself may be affected by changes in financial policy, because such changes may not be offset on personal account. Consequently, the investment opportunity set available to investors may be altered by corporate financial policies, although firms of the same operating risk class are valued identically in the market place. One obvious difference between personal borrowing and corporate borrowing is the existence of corporate *limited liability*, which is crucial once we allow for the possibility of default risk.

Stiglitz (see footnote 8) suggests a mechanism to establish the MM theorem under conditions of default risk. That is, a financial intermediary can be created that can reconstitute any firm that alters its debt-to-equity ratio. This intermediary purchases all of the bonds and shares of the firm and reissues bonds and shares in exactly the same ratio as in the original equilibrium. Thus, if the intermediary can be created *costlessly*, the opportunity set facing investors is unchanged, and the firm's debt policy is again inconsequential.

However, Stiglitz's financial intermediation proof raises an interesting question. Why don't investors themselves replicate the financial intermediary? For instance, investors owning the same proportion of each of the firm's bonds and stock have a direct share in the firm's activities. They can then use their holdings as exclusive collateral and issue the same sort of securities as the financial intermediary. Recall that this may not be possible, because the intermediary is a firm subject to limited liability. However, if the limited liability provisions can be included in the securities issued by investors as well, we will have "equal access" to the capital market by both investors and firms.

The notion of equal access as defined by Fama[11] is really equivalent to Stiglitz's notion of the costless financial intermediary. Thus, both notions are mechanisms intended to establish perfect substitutability of homemade leverage for corporate leverage. Indeed, the critical assumption (and the only one!) needed for the MM theorem is that investors and firms compete equally in the financial markets. Of course, a firm may enjoy monopoly power in the real sector with payoff

---

[10] See D. Baron, "Default Risk, Home-Made Leverage and the Modigliani-Miller Theorem," *American Economic Review* (March 1974). Note that we are dealing with default risk or bankruptcy *per se* and not with *costs* associated with it. These costs are subjects of Chapter 4.

[11] E. Fama, "The Effects of a Firm's Investment and Financing Decisions on the Welfare of its Securityholders," *American Economic Review* (June 1978).

streams that cannot be replicated by other firms. However, once the firm chooses its investment strategies, it can do nothing through its financing decisions to alter the opportunity set facing investors. Investors can compete equally in the financial markets by issuing the same kind of securities against their holdings in the firms that firms can themselves issue.[12]

2.3 Debt and Taxes

Up to this point we have assumed that both corporate income and personal income are untaxed. However, death and taxes, as they say, are a matter of certainty. For our purpose, taxes pose a friction and thereby contaminate the original clean MM environment. This environmental factor may establish a role for corporate financial policy. Indeed, the U.S. tax code is discriminatory in its treatment of bond income and equity income both at the level of recipients and payers. Corporations are allowed to deduct interest payments in computing their taxable income, but payments on equity capital, such as dividends, are disallowed as a deduction. On the other hand, capital gains, an important component of equity income, are subject to taxation only upon realization. Unrealized capital gains are a means of obtaining interest-free government loans. Even when they are realized, they are taxed at a preferential rate in comparison with interest income and dividend income. To complicate matters, tax treatment of investment income varies across national boundaries, hence making it difficult to generate an internationally accepted theory of corporate finance under taxation. Nonetheless, the MM theorem's implication that financial mix has no *inherent* value is universal; it has no national boundary. In what follows, we will focus on the U.S. tax environment and its implications for corporate finance.

2.31 Debt and Corporate Income Taxes

Suppose that we maintain the same assumptions as in (2.21) but that corporate income is taxed at a *uniform* marginal rate with tax

---

[12] Bankruptcy introduces an additional phenomenon into the picture. Although the firm may not affect its total value, its new financing decisions can redistribute wealth among the existing securityholders. For example, an additional debt increases the default probability with the consequent decrease in bond value and the commensurate increase in equity value. E. Fama and M. Miller, in *The Theory of Finance* (Hinsdale, Ill.: Holt, Rinehart and Winston, Inc., 1972) suggest "me-first rules" through which the securityholders protect themselves from one another and from the effects of new financing decisions. However, Fama (see footnote 11) argues accurately that with "equal access," these rules are unnecessary when expropriative contracts are *rationally* priced in the market. Much the same point is made in footnote 4 of R. Haugen and L. Senbet, "The Insignificance of Bankruptcy Costs to the Theory of Optimal Capital Structure," *Journal of Finance* (May 1978).

deductibility of interest payments. The assumption of uniformity is close to reality. The marginal corporate tax rate is uniform across all taxable corporations for which the taxable federal income exceeds $100,000. Currently, the corporate tax rate is 46 percent at the federal level plus the applicable state tax rate. Now if we denote the tax rate as τ_C, we can create two portfolio strategies generating identical after-tax return streams as shown in Table 2.2.

TABLE 2.2

	Net Investment	*Return Stream*
Strategy A [Hold α fraction of the levered firm's stock]	αS_L	$\alpha(\tilde{X}_L - rD)(1 - \tau_C)$
Strategy B [Hold α fraction of the unlevered firm's stock and borrow $\alpha D(1 - \tau_C)$ on personal account]	$\alpha[V_U - D(1 - \tau_C)]$	$\alpha(\tilde{X}_U - rD)(1 - \tau_C)$

Strategies A and B yield identical return patterns. In conformity to the law of one price, the net investment should be identical so that

$$\alpha S_L = \alpha[V_U - D(1 - \tau_C)]$$

Hence,

$$S_L + D = V_L = V_U + \tau_C D \tag{7}$$

The value of the levered firm is no longer identical to the unlevered firm. It exceeds its unlevered counterpart by what amounts to a government subsidy, $\tau_C D$. Indeed, the value of the firm is maximized at a *corner* in which debt financing completely dominates equity financing.[13] Let us again examine briefly the sense in which debt financing enhances the value of the levered firm. The *before tax* pie, X, is still unaffected by financing decisions, but the *after tax* pie is increased in the sense shown in Table 2.3.

---

[13] The impact of tax subsidy on the levered stock price per share can easily be shown by using the same reasoning as in subsection (2.22). If the firm retires M shares of equity at P_L by using the proceeds from the issuance of $D = MP_L$.

$$S_L = (N - M)P_L = V_L - D = V_U + \tau_C D = NP_U + \tau_C D - D$$

Therefore,

$$NP_L = NP_U + \tau_C D$$

Thus,

$$P_L = P_U + \frac{\tau_C D}{N}$$

TABLE 2.3 Payoffs to Claimholders

| | Payoffs to Claimholders | | | Aggregate Payoff to Capital Contributors |
	Debt-holders	Equityholders	Govern-ment	
The Unlevered Firm	—	$\tilde{X}(1 - \tau_C)$	$\tau_C\tilde{X}$	$\tilde{X}(1 - \tau_C)$
The Levered Firm	rD	$(\tilde{X} - rD)(1 - \tau_C)$	$\tau(\tilde{X} - rD)$	$\tilde{X}(1 - \tau_C) + \tau_C rD$

The tax subsidy in (7) reflects the discounted value of the incremental payoff, $\tau_C rD$, as shown in the preceding table. The model holds true because the government is treated as being *exogenous* to the system. If the government wishes to recoup its revenue loss, though, it can presumably raise taxes, which are borne by the society at large. If the corporate sector were to take the brunt of the tax recoup, the aggregate value of the corporate sector would be maintained at the level of the value of the unlevered component prior to the tax increase. Nonetheless, the structure of the model in (7) and the financing policy are still unaffected. That is, a particular firm would still go to a corner in its choice of debt financing. This corner solution is obviously unattractive in the light of interior mixes of debt and equity financing observed in the real world. Moreover, certain regularities are observed in industry-based patterns of financing. However, we have not yet accommodated an additional feature of the U.S. tax code, namely, personal income taxation. This is the subject of the next subsection.

MILLER(1977) **2.32 Debt, Corporate Income Taxes, and Personal Income Taxes**

Suppose that personal taxation is *uniform* across all investors but differential between bond and equity incomes. Let τ_{ps} and τ_{pb} denote personal tax rates on income from stocks and income from bonds, respectively. Again, we can posit two portfolio strategies resulting in identical income streams.

TABLE 2.4

	Net Investment	Return Stream
Strategy A [Hold α fraction of the levered firm's stock]	αS_L	$\alpha(\tilde{X} - rD)$ $(1 - \tau_C)(1 - \tau_{ps})$
Strategy B {Hold α fraction of the unlevered firm's stock and borrow $\alpha[D(1 - \tau_C)(1 - \tau_{ps})/ (1 - \tau_{pb})]$}	$\alpha\left[V_U - \dfrac{D(1 - \tau_C)(1 - \tau_{ps})}{1 - \tau_{pb}}\right]$	$\alpha(\tilde{X} - rD)$ $(1 - \tau_C)(1 - \tau_{ps})$

Again, by the law of one price, the two strategies should be worth the same so that

$$\alpha S_L = \alpha \left[V_U - \frac{D(1 - \tau_C)(1 - \tau_{ps})}{1 - \tau_{pb}} \right]$$

Hence,

$$S_L + D = V_L = V_U + D \left[1 - \frac{(1 - \tau_C)(1 - \tau_{ps})}{1 - \tau_{pb}} \right] \qquad (8)$$

The last term in (8) is the tax subsidy. It converges to the subsidy in (7), $\tau_C D$, if bond and equity incomes are taxed identically at the personal level (i.e., if $\tau_{ps} = \tau_{pb}$). On the other hand, if the debt income is taxed at a higher rate (i.e., $\tau_{pb} > \tau_{ps}$), the subsidy falls below the traditional value, $\tau_C D$, and it could even conceivably be transformed into a government penalty, depending upon the parameters employed.

Interpretations = MM '63

We wish to provide the following numerical example to illustrate the tax effects of debt financing, assuming perpetuity.

$\tau_C = 50\% = $ the uniform corporate tax rate

$\tau_{pb} = 40\% = $ the uniform personal tax rate on bond income

$\tau_{ps} = 20\% = $ the uniform personal tax rate on equity income

$D = \$500,000 = $ corporate debt financing at interest rate, r_C, of 10%

Pro Forma Income Statement

	The Unlevered Firm	The Levered Firm
Expected Operating Income ($\bar{X}$)	200,000	200,000
Interest Expense ($r_C D$)	0	50,000
Pre-Tax Income	200,000	150,000
Tax	100,000	75,000
Net Income	100,000	75,000
After-Tax Income to Capital Contributors		
Equityholders	80,000	60,000
Bondholders	0	30,000
Total	80,000	90,000
Tax Subsidy	0	(10,000)
	80,000	80,000

Suppose that the unlevered cost of capital, K_U, is 16%. Then, V_L = V_U + present value of the tax subsidy = 80,000/.16 + 10,000/.06 = 500,000 + 166,667 = $666,667. You can also verify the answer by plugging in the relevant parameters in equation (8). Note also that the maximum value of the tax subsidy occurs when either (a) there is no personal taxation or when (b) there is personal tax symmetry in that $\tau_{ps} = \tau_{pb}$. Thus, the tax subsidy to debt financing occurs due to asymmetric treatment of tax deductions on corporate capital. At any rate, you can verify that the maximum tax subsidy in either case is $\tau_{c}D = \$250,000$.

The tax subsidy diminishes as the tax rate on equity income, τ_{ps}, approaches zero. The subsidy disappears altogether when $(1 - \tau_C)(1 - \tau_{ps}) = 1 - \tau_{pb}$, and if τ_{ps} is assumed zero, this condition requires that $\tau_C = \tau_{pb}$. If so, personal leverage is a perfect substitute for corporate leverage, and the Modigliani-Miller theorem is restored for this special case. Corporations and individual investors are again on an equal footing! This result reminds us of an important condition for the irrelevance of corporate financial policy. It is not the existence of taxes *per se* that matters to corporate debt policy but whether or not taxes are *discriminatory* in treating corporate debt and personal debt. On the other hand, one would expect the more realistic case of *progressive* income taxation together with corporate taxation to create substantial distortion in the financial system. This is the subject of the following subsection.

2.33 The Miller Bond Market Equilibrium

Merton Miller presented an insightful and controversial presidential address at the 1976 meeting of the American Finance Association. The title of the speech is "Debt and Taxes," and it is by far the most heavily cited presidential address in this field.[14] Unlike his coauthored work with Franco Modigliani in 1963 and another painstaking empirical work in 1966 in which he corroborated this tax effect,[15] Miller now argues that debt policy is a matter of indifference to an individual firm, although there is an optimal aggregate level of debt for the corporate sector as a whole. Miller reaches this conclusion under the following assumptions: (a) progressive personal tax rates reach a maximum at a level beyond the corporate tax rate; (b) no tax avoidance

---

[14] Although the germ for the paper originates from D. Farrar and L. L. Selwyn, "Taxes, Corporate Financial Policy and the Returns to Investors," *National Tax Journal* (December 1967), M. Miller's "Debt and Taxes," *Journal of Finance* (May 1977), a decade later, has opened up a large volume of new research. In this sense, it has played a similar role as the classic MM (1958) paper. Nonetheless, it is fair to mention that Miller's results were anticipated in J. Stiglitz, "Taxation, Corporate Financial Policy, and the Cost of Capital," *Journal of Public Economics* (February 1973).

[15] M. Miller and F. Modigliani, "Some Estimates of the Cost of Capital to the Electric Utility Industry, 1954–57," *American Economic Review* (June 1966). At the time, this was perhaps the most extensive and carefully designed empirical work offered in support of the 1963 MM tax-adjusted valuation model. Now, given Miller (1977), it no longer holds true.

or arbitrage schemes are allowed for both individuals and firms; (c) there is a personal tax rate differential in favor of income from stocks $T_{ps} < T_{pB}$ as compared with income from bonds; and (d) the opportunity for riskless borrowing and lending exists.[16,17]

To explain the Miller (1977) equilibrium, it is helpful to go back to MM (1958) and MM (1963) and posit them graphically. The MM (1958) position is that investors and firms are on an equal footing in transforming the unlevered security into debt and levered equity. In other words, homemade leverage is a perfect substitute for corporate leverage. Consider Figure 2.1, which measures the aggregate quantity of corporate debt along the horizontal axis and the certainty-equiv-alent rate of interest along the vertical axis in 2.1(A). The correspond-ing valuation of the corporate sector is plotted along the vertical axis in 2.1(B). The supply curve is perfectly elastic through r*, or equiv-alently through V_U, the value of the unlevered counterpart of the corporate sector, as the sector continues to be more levered. The infinite elasticity stems from the fact that corporations can costlessly transform their all-equity positions into any degree of leverage, so long as one form of financing engenders identical cost (r*) as any other form. On the other hand, the demand curve is also perfectly elastic because investors can duplicate the same transformation on a personal account. Hence, investors do not accept interest rate (yield) differentials across securities. Thus, the supply and demand curves overlap each other. The MM (1958) is a statement of this overlap leading to *indeterminate* leverage ratio either at a particular firm level or at the level of the corporate sector as a whole. Now you can see that the MM theorem is valid for any mix of securities, including complex financial instruments, such as convertible bonds, callable bonds, preferred stock, warrants, etc. Any corporate financial transformation (e.g., corporate leverage) can be duplicated by personal financial transformation (e.g., homemade leverage) leading to corporate fi-nancial *indeterminacy* at the individual and aggregate levels. Accord-

---

[16] Assumptions (a), (b) and (d) are relaxed in later chapters, and Miller's conclusions are shown to be robust except in the case of debt-related costs such as agency costs and unutilized corporate tax shelters. Miller focuses on tax exposure by ignoring the consequences of risk exposure. The latter is particularly important when the capital market is incomplete in the sense that securities do not exist so as to span all the possible contingencies. Recently, Taggart, in "Taxes and Corporate Capital Structure in an Incomplete Market," *Journal of Finance* (June 1980), has extended the Miller analysis into an incomplete market. He shows that the capital structure irrelevance proposition holds under the Miller tax environment with an additional restriction that investors sort themselves into extreme leverage clienteles.

[17] The progressive tax specification in Miller (1977) is not entirely consistent with the U.S. tax code, however, in that taxation is progressive across investment *groups*. Pro-gressive taxation within each group, as a function of *taxable income*, would require a more stringent set of conditions for debt neutrality. See R. Dammon, "Portfolio Se-lection, Capital Structure, and Taxes," Wisconsin Working Paper (April 1984).

ing to the MM theorem changes in corporate financial structure over time are merely random occurrences.

The horizontal supply and demand curves are no longer overlapping in a tax world with taxes. The MM (1963) allows only for corporate taxation, and hence breaking perfect substitution between corporate debt and personal debt. In that the supply curve is horizontal through $r^*/(1 - \tau_C)$, the rate of interest which would pass through the full tax subsidy to bondholders. Therefore, the supply curve makes an upward parallel shift in 2.1(A). It is parallel, because corporations are still assumed to perform costless financial transformation. The *marginal* tax subsidy is independent of the extent of transformation (or financial leverage). However, the demand curve is still flat through r^*. Thus, in the MM (1963) world, it pays to move to a corner solution in which the entire corporate sector is levered at nearly 100 percent debt-to-equity ratio. Corporate leverage is a superior substitute for personal leverage.

If we consider personal taxation, we enter the world of Miller (1977). The MM (1963) supply curve is still maintained through $r^*/(1 - \tau_C)$. They are willing to pay $(r^*\tau_C)/(1 - \tau_C)$ as a premium on the debt that they issue, because of tax deductibility of interest payments. Personal taxation of bond interest implies that the demand curve cannot be flat through r^* for taxable investors. It is upward sloping to entice investors in progressively higher tax brackets. The initial horizontal stretch through r^* is the demand for corporate bonds by tax-exempt individuals and organizations. A taxable individual with the marginal tax rate τ_{pb}^i will be indifferent between tax-exempt securities and corporate bonds only if $r_C = r^*/(1 - \tau_{pb}^i)$. Indeed, equilibrium occurs when this point of indifference on the demand curve is exactly matched by firms on the supply side. Thus, equilibrium occurs at the point of intersection between the supply and demand curves when enough debt (i.e., D*) has been issued to drive the rate of interest to $r_C = r^*/(1 - \tau_C)$. While an optimal amount of debt capital exists in an aggregate, economywide sense, any individual firm is indifferent to the amount of debt in its capital structure.

Conclusion

2.34 Equilibrium Properties

2.341 FURTHER IMPLICIT CONDITIONS

There are three additional implicit conditions in the graphic analysis of the preceding Miller equilibrium. First, tax arbitrage or avoidance schemes are sufficiently restricted that investors cannot mitigate the differential tax consequences of various securities. For instance, they cannot eliminate their tax liabilities by borrowing to hold tax-exempt securities. Nor do they engage in large-scale shortselling of corporate securities for tax arbitrage purposes. Thus, a tax-induced yield differential develops between corporate debt and corporate stock that is based on the corporate tax rate (or higher if stock income is taxed as argued below). However, a yield differential of such a magnitude as that implied in the Miller equilibrium is not empirically supported, as we will argue later in the book. The tax arbitrage restriction is crucial and its implications for the bond market equilibrium are developed in Chapter 7.

Throughout the Miller analysis debt is presumed riskless, or if it is risky the attendant agency problems are costlessly resolved. In the presence of agency problems, which are the subject of this book, corporations are no longer able to perform costless financial transformation. This assumption has a crucial impact on the elasticity of the supply curve. Chapter 7 explores the implications of agency problems for the Miller equilibrium.

The third assumption implicit in Figure 2.1 is that equity is tax-exempt (i.e., $\tau_{ps} = 0$). Tax-exemption assumption is closer to reality if all of equity income is generated through capital gains. Capital gains are taxed at a preferential rate as opposed to dividends, and they are untaxed until realized. Investors can preserve their consumption pattern by borrowing against the full value of equity with unrealized capital gains. You can also give away equity with unrealized capital gains in charitable contributions for its full value. Thus, it can be said that the portion of income represented by capital gains is nearly tax-exempt. On the other hand, if equity income is represented totally by dividend income, then equity ceases to exist in the Miller equilibrium. This is because taxable investors would demand the same rate of interest as bonds, but corporations would be unwilling to supply equity since equity income is not *tax deductible*. Therefore, under this extreme case we see that the Miller (1977) equilibrium swings to the same corner as the MM (1963) model with the corporate sector being levered at nearly 100 percent debt-to-equity ratio.

However, equity income is normally observed as a composite of both capital gains and dividend income. The tax rate on such a composite security is a weighted average of the tax rate on the fully taxable dividend income and the *effective* rate on capital gains. The effective rate on the latter is reduced significantly depending upon the extent to which capital gains are deferred for tax purposes. Thus, there ought to be some average tax rate on equity income that sustains the Miller equilibrium so that financial leverage is still inconsequential at a particular firm level. In this context, the fully taxable securities (bonds), the preferentially taxable securities (stocks), and the tax-exempt securities (municipal bonds) may coexist in the Miller bond market equilibrium.[18]

---

[18] See R. Haugen, L. Senbet, and E. Talmor, "Debt, Dividends, and Taxes," Wisconsin Working Paper (July 1984).

Figure 2.1. The Bond Market Equilibrium

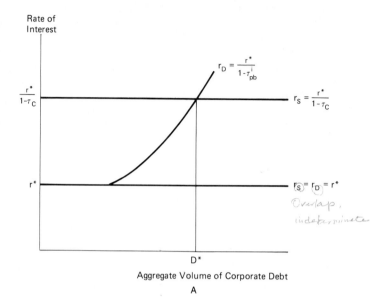

Rate of
Interest

$r_D = \dfrac{r^*}{1-\tau^i_{pb}}$

$\dfrac{r^*}{1-\tau_C}$

$r_S = \dfrac{r^*}{1-\tau_C}$

r^*

$r_S = r_D = r^*$

Overlap,
indeterminate

D*

Aggregate Volume of Corporate Debt

A

Aggregate Value of
the Corporate Sector

$V_L = V_U + \tau_C D$
[MM, 1963]

[Miller, 1977]

$V_L = V_U$
[MM, 1958]

$V_L = V_U + D[1 - \dfrac{(1-\tau_C)}{(1-\tau^i_{pb})}]$

D*

Aggregate Volume of Corporate Debt

B

The issue of equity income taxation has taken on particular significance since the new tax provision on investment income was initiated
by the Reagan administration. This provision reduces the maximum
ordinary tax rate on investment income from 70 percent to 50 percent.
This may create a tax subsidy of corporate debt financing unless state
income taxes do not sufficiently augment the federal income taxation
to retain the Miller equilibrium. To see this, suppose that $\tau_{ps} = 20\%$,
$\tau_C = 50\%$, $r^* = 10\%$. The break-even supply interest rate that reduces
capital structure indifference is $r_C^{supply} = r^*/(1 - \tau_C)(1 - \tau_{ps}) = 25\%$.
This implies that the supply curve in Figure 2.1 shifts upward from
$\left(\dfrac{r^*}{1 - \tau_C}\right)$ to $\dfrac{r^*}{(1 - \tau_C)(1 - \tau_{ps})}$, but the demand curve under the new
tax rule may not intersect. For this particular numerical example, the
implicit personal tax rate, τ_{pb}^*, is 60 percent, which is 10 percent above
the new maximum tax rate on investment income. Of course, this
numerical example ignores the impact of state income taxation on
τ_{pb}, but it suggests that the effect of the new Reagan tax policy may
be to restore a tax subsidy of corporate debt financing in many instances.

2.342 FINANCIAL CLIENTELES

In a complete certainty (or a complete market) framework, the
equilibrium implies that corporate bonds are held only by investors
in low tax brackets ($\tau_{pb}^i < \tau_C$), and equity and tax-exempt securities
are held by high tax bracket investors. Thus, portfolio holdings are
specialized or polarized under conditions of certainty or sufficient
market completeness allowing for the creation of any desired risk
exposure for a given tax bracket.

Now suppose that you desire to hold an appropriately diversified
portfolio under conditions of uncertainty. Then you are left with
trading off tax exposure with risk exposure if markets are incomplete
in the sense that you cannot create any arbitrary return pattern while
simultaneously tailoring it to your personal tax situation. For instance,
low tax groups must hold *risky* corporate stock if they wish to hold
any risky assets. In this case, any firm capital structure is no longer
as good as any other for a particular investor because as Taggart (see
footnote 16) argues, the bond market equilibrium is preserved only
in the sense that firms adopt either highly levered or highly unlevered
capital structures. Thus, investors sort themselves into leverage clienteles, and portfolios are less specialized than in the previous case. Now
clienteles form for corporate stock in the following sense, assuming
again zero taxation on equity income for expositional purposes.

TABLE 2.5

Leverage	Net Investment	Return Stream
Corporate Leverage	αS_L	$\alpha(X - r_C D)(1 - \tau_C)$
Personal Leverage	$\alpha(S_U - D)$	$\alpha[X(1 - \tau_C) - r_C D(1 - \tau_{pb}^i)]$

Note that, given the Miller equilibrium, the net investment is the same for both strategies. That is, you pay the same amount (αS_L) when you purchase the levered stock or *borrow through the firm* to buy the stock as when you purchase the unlevered stock and borrow on your personal account. That is, $S_U - D = S_L$ or $V_U = V_L = D + S_L$ in equilibrium as determined at the margin by the intersection point in I(A) or in I(B) in Figure 2.1. However, your tax status may be below or above the intersection point, and that determines your portfolio choice. Clearly, in Table 2.5, if your tax rate (τ_{pb}^i) is below the corporate tax rate (τ_C) you are better off with corporate leverage. The return stream generated by the expedient of borrowing through the firm dominates the alternative return stream through your personal leverage. Of course, the reverse is true if your tax rate is above the corporate tax rate. Suppose that $X = \$10$ million, $\alpha = .01$, $\tau_C = 50\%$, $r_C = 20\%$, $D = \$5$ million. If $\tau_{pb} = 40\%$, your return is \$44,000 via personal leverage while it is \$46,000 if $\tau_{pb} = 60\%$. Consequently, you opt for personal leverage if you are in a 60% tax bracket, and you opt for corporate leverage if you are in a 40% tax bracket. Thus, high tax groups gravitate to unlevered firms and low tax groups gravitate to levered firms, and, in this sense, we have empirically tractable financial clienteles for corporate stock. Unfortunately, it is dangerous to conduct empirical investigation at this stage, because tax arbitrage opportunities and the attendant costs must be carefully taken into account to generalize the theory. This is the subject of Chapter 7.

financial clienteles

2.4 Conclusion

The contribution of the Modigliani-Miller theorem is that value cannot be created by rearranging capital structure. That is, capital structure *per se* has no intrinsic value. In the Modigliani-Miller world, investment and financing decisions are completely separable. Their theorem is shown to hold under generalized uncertainty. However, imperfections, such as taxes, may create a positive role for corporate finance. Even in the tax world, though, the *limited* Modigliani-Miller theorem established by Miller (1977) suggests that capital structure is still indeterminate at the individual firm level although it is determinate at the level of the corporate sector as a whole. Thus, taxes alone may be unable to explain observed financial regularities and complexities. The purpose of this book is, of course, to fill this void by introducing agency problems as a basis for corporate finance. Chapter 3 discusses the nature of such agency problems.

The Nature of Agency Problems

3.1 Introduction

Delegation of decision-making authority is an essential feature of the modern corporation. Securityholders delegate authority to professionals who have managerial skills. Securityholders differ in terms of risk sharing depending upon their mode of ownership. Equityholders in a given firm bear more risk than bondholders of the same firm. In the tradition of finance, management is presumed to operate as a delegate to equityholders who bear residual risk. Bondholders, in turn, have recourse to equityholders. Delegation of decision-making authority may give rise to conflicts of interest between agents (managers, existing stockholders) and principals (providers of new capital).

Agency problems emerge when conflicts of interest between agents and principals or among the principals themselves affect the operation of the business enterprise. Our analysis of agency problems is based on two fundamental behavioral assumptions. First, all individuals are assumed to choose actions that maximize their own personal welfare. As a consequence, as decision-making authority is delegated by principals to agents, agents use this power to promote their own well-being. Actions that are chosen by agents to achieve this goal may or may not be in the best interests of principals. Second, individuals are

25

assumed to be rational and capable of forming unbiased expectations regarding the impact of agency problems and the associated future value of their wealth. Rationality implies that every individual recognizes the self-interest motivations of all others so that future decisions by agents based on their own interests are anticipated and taken into account by principals.

The economic theory of agency focuses on the relationship between a single principal who provides capital and consequently possesses a claim on the end-of-period value of the firm and an agent (manager) whose efforts are needed to produce this value. The financial theory of agency focuses on the relationships between different groups of securityholders (equity and bondholders) in the context of optimal financing of the firm. In this chapter, we identify agency problems that appear in the economic and financial literature utilizing a unified framework. The potential power of these agency problems to rationalize and explain complex financial contracts, complex financial structures, and relative prices of financial claims is evaluated in later chapters.

3.2 The Economic Theory of Agency

The standard economic theory of agency considers two individuals— a principal who provides the capital and an agent (manager) who provides the effort. Both are assumed to be expected utility maximizers. Principals value end-of-period wealth, which is derived from their share in the realized value of the firm. Agents value their end-of-period wealth stemming from their share in the value of the firm and their work (effort), which is a factor in the firm's production function. Agency problems arise because, under the behavioral assumption of self-interest, agents do not invest their best efforts unless such investment is consistent with maximizing their own welfare. The agency model is basically a formulation of the principal's problem of choosing the "best" employment contract for the agent. "Best" is defined in the context of Pareto-optimality. A Pareto-optimal contract is such that no other contract can improve the welfare of one party without reducing the welfare of the other. Such a contract is presumed to be self-enforcing when the effort is unobservable. However, a forcing contract can be designed if efforts are fully observable (see below). Observability of the agent's effort is really the core of the incentive problem in the economic theory of agency, as well as in the financial theory of agency. It is sometimes tempting to think that observability of the end-of-period value is equivalent to observability of the effort level. But this is false. While the effort level *affects* the level of output of the firm (i.e., the end-of-period value or cash flows), the output is also governed by other *random events* that are beyond the control of the agent. An agency problem arises when the consequences of the agent's effort cannot be distinguished entirely from the consequences of other random events by observing output alone. In the tradition of the economic theory of agency, the output (pay-off) level is mutually observable by the principal and the agent, but the effort level is observable only by the agent. Although the effort level is not observable by the principal, an attempt to mitigate the cost arising from the agency problem calls for a design of a contract or a sharing rule that provides the right incentive for the agent to provide the optimal effort. Such a contract is *self-enforcing*, because it is in the agent's best interest to perform. On the other hand, a *forcing* contract can be used in the event that the effort level is fully observable. In this case there will be an explicit penalty imposed on the agent if the desired effort is not provided. Both types of contract must depend on parameters that are jointly observed, including the realization of output or the end-of-period value of the firm, so that pay-offs to the parties are observed and determined without ambiguity.

Enforceable contracts specify without ambiguity the share of each party in the observed value of the firm. Since the end-of-period value of the firm is uncertain at the time contracts are signed, the contractual distribution of this value between the principal and the agent implies a given risk sharing between the two. For example, a contract that provides a constant dollar compensation for the agent implies that all the risk is imposed on the principal. A contract that provides a constant dollar compensation to the principal (i.e., partial financing of the firm by riskless bonds) implies that all the risk is borne by the agent.

From its beginning, the economic literature on agency has searched for contracts that are "first-best." First-best contracts motivate the agent to invest an optimal amount of effort. That is, they solve the incentive problem and at the same time produce an optimal distribution of the risk between the principal and the agent. First-best contracts must provide a solution to the incentive problem as if the risk sharing problem did not exist and simultaneously a solution to the risk sharing problem as if the incentive problem did not exist.[1]

Before proceeding into the analysis of each problem, we will summarize the framework that characterizes most of the economic research in this area. First, the analysis is based on a single period model. This is a limiting assumption, because it ignores the implications of the outcomes in one period on the structure of contracts in future periods. As we shall see below, the learning process of market participants, which is embedded in multiperiod analysis, gives rise to "goodwill" and human capital, which affect the actions of agents and generally mitigate agency problems.[2] Second, the analysis is based on one agent and one principal. Except for the introduction of a reservation

---

[1] The contracting literature is cited in footnote 1 of Chapter 6.
[2] There is now a growing attempt to deal with multiperiod aspects of agency problems. See, for instance, R. Lambert, "Managerial Incentives in Multiperiod Agency Relationships," Ph.D. dissertation, Stanford University, 1982.

(minimum) utility level that must be satisfied to attract agents, the analysis ignores the existence of markets and the implications of competition among principals and agents. Third, the analysis assumes that the manager's preferences and action alternatives are perfectly known to principals. Fourth, the analysis assumes that the end-of-period wealth of both parties is limited to the realized value of the analyzed firm. The possibilities for diversifying via the capital market, and thereby reducing the amount of risk that is shared, are generally ignored. Fifth, the analysis assumes that contracts are binding, which implies that any commitment in an enforceable contract is perfectly honored. That is, the possibility of default on the part of either principals or agents is ignored.

3.21 The Nature of the Incentive Problem in the Principal-Agent Relationship

As mentioned above, recent research in this area specifies the agents' utility as a function of their end-of-period wealth *and* the amount of effort they invest in the firm. Effort is assumed to generate disutility to the agent. On the other hand, effort contributes to the output of the firm. The principals' problem is to design a compensation package that motivates managers (agents) to employ their best efforts. The output of the firm is assumed to be a function of managerial efforts and a (random) realized state of the world which is beyond the control of principals and agents.

In this framework, are we able to structure contracts that will motivate managers to invest the appropriate effort? As is shown in the literature, such contracts are feasible if either managerial efforts or the state of the world can be unambiguously identified at the end of the period. Suppose that managerial efforts can be measured. A simple contract that relates compensation to actual efforts is sufficient to motivate managers to work. Alternatively, a contract in which managers agree to pay penalties if their efforts are below a given benchmark will fulfill the same motivational function. Unambiguous observation on the realized state of the world is also sufficient to establish contracts that assure appropriate investment of efforts. Such observation, coupled with the exact specification of the production function, enables the principal to derive the actual effort and to enforce contracts based on actual efforts.

Complications in structuring contracts arise whenever efforts or states of the world are unobservable. Suppose that the only observable variable is the firm's actual output. It is impossible to distinguish whether a low level of output is the result of insufficient effort or the result of an unfavorable state of the world. While motivation can be established if the manager is the sole residual claimant of the firm's output (i.e., financing by risk-free debt), such solutions have drawbacks because they impose unwarranted risk on the management. This is the particular case for which only *second best* contracts are feasible.

Second best contracts are defined as contracts that are best relative
to the amount of information available for inclusion in the contract.
Full information (i.e., information on firm's output, agents' efforts,
or the state of the world) enable the construction of first best contracts.
Limited information (i.e., information on a firm's output and possibly
on variables that serve as proxies for agents' efforts or the state of
the world) produce contracts that are inferior to first best contracts.
Among those contracts, and subject to the availability of information,
second best contracts are optimal. Obviously, second best contracts
can be improved if innovation in the structure of contracts or the
production of better information proxies become cost-efficient. This
is the context in which progress in the production of detailed audited
accounting information may play an important role in mitigating the
incentive problem (see Chapter 8).

3.22 Risk Sharing by Principals and Agents

The sharing of risk among principals and agents is a central issue
in an agency problem. Early studies, which ignored the incentive
problem, were able to produce optimal risk sharing contracts that
were based on the risk aversion parameters of the principal and agent.
In later studies, it was shown that contracts that provide appropriate
incentives may cause substantial reduction in the welfare of agents by
burdening them with most of the underlying risk. Optimal risk sharing
is a simple problem when at least one of the parties is risk neutral.
That party takes all the risk. However, when both parties are risk
averse and the incentive problem is not solved through complete
observations of the agents' effort, only second best contracts are feasible. The issue of risk sharing is further complicated if we recognize
that the principal and the agent have access to other capital investments. This is a very recent extension of the agency models and its
implications are yet to be developed.

Analytical solutions to the problem of risk sharing are greatly simplified under explicit assumptions regarding the utility functons of
the parties involved and the underlying distribution of asset returns.
It is common to assume, in a single period context, that both principals
and agents behave according to an exponential utility function $U(X)$
$= 1 - e^{-AX}$. It is well known that since this particular functon exhibits
constant absolute risk aversion, the optimal fractional sharing rule
does not depend on outcome and is given by $S_p = A_a/(A_a + A_p)$,
where S_p is the share of the principal in any outcome and A_a and A_p
are the absolute risk aversion parameters of the agent and the principal, respectively.[3] It is clear that if the solution for the incentive
problem is to let the agents bear the consequences of their efforts

---

[3] A formal derivation of this sharing rule can be obtained from the authors upon
request.

(i.e., issuing risk free debt), risk sharing will not be optimal unless the
agents are risk neutral.

Further simplification of the risk sharing problem is obtained when
the underlying asset returns follow particular distributions. For example, if the underlying distribution is normal and if only *linear* sharing rules are considered, risk can be analyzed in terms of the variance
alone.[4] This is important because nonpolynomial (e.g., nonquadratic)
utility functions produce complicated risk measures when the underlying distribution is not normal. Analysis of the risk sharing problem
may require a consideration of all the moments (including skewness,
etc.) of the distribution. The assumption of a linear sharing rule is
required to ensure that normal distribution of pay-offs is preserved
for each of the parties involved. It is well known that any linear
function of a normal variate is also normal.

A second example that allows for the development of first best
contracts is the case of a uniform distribution. If the extreme values
of this distribution are known to the parties, they can design contracts
which, in particular cases, may solve the incentive problem of optimal
sharing of risk. To see this, consider a case where managerial efforts
tend to shift the mean of the distribution without affecting the variance. This is demonstrated in Figure 3.1. Suppose that high managerial effort produces a distribution of returns, EFGH, with a mean

Figure 3.1. Risk Sharing Under a Uniform Distribution

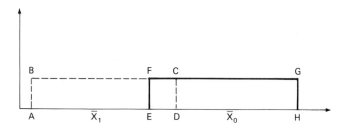

of $\overline{X}_0$. If the manager invests only low effort, the distribution will shift
to ABCD with a mean $\overline{X}_1$. It is possible to consider a contract in which
the manager will pay a severe penalty if the final outcome is below
E. Subject to this penalty, risk can be shared according to any mutual
agreement based on the distribution EFGH. The penalty assures that
the manager will invest the effort. The distributional property is such
that the consequences of the effort can be observed, and hence a
forcing contract with a penalty function can be designed.

---

[4] Linear sharing rules are rules that share the output in constant proportions. Unlevered equity and risk-free debt, as we know them, are consistent with linear sharing
rules. Options, however, produce nonlinear sharing rules, as the proportion of the
output received by the holder of an option depends on the outcome.

3.3 The Financial Theory of Agency[5]

The financial theory of agency can be considered as an application of the economic theory of agency to contractual relationships in finance. Nonetheless, its primary distinctive feature is an explicit consideration of financial markets. Agency problems that are considered in the financial literature originate from three sources. First, partial ownership of the firm by owner-managers may provide an incentive to consume nonpecuniary benefits or perquisites beyond that which a sole owner would consume optimally. Second, the existence of debt financing under limited liability creates an incentive to stockholders to engage in high-risk activities that transfer wealth from bondholders to stockholders. Limited liability on previously issued debt may cause stockholders to forgo new profitable investments. Also, it may reduce the value of the firm when stockholder-bondholder disputes are resolved through the process of costly bankruptcy. Third, there is the problem of informational asymmetry. The problem arises when management, which is presumed to be acting in the interests of existing securityholders, attempts to raise additional capital from outsiders. Management possesses inside information on the future values of the firm, but it cannot convey the information to the market unambiguously because of a moral hazard problem. If management sells the securities to outsiders at undervalued prices, existing securityholders suffer a loss that can be viewed as an agency cost.

The above classification of agency problems is based on their origin. A related classification emphasizes the financial asset (equity or debt) that is subject to a particular agency problem. The agency problems of equity are associated with informational asymmetry and excessive "perquisite" consumption. The agency problems of debt are associated with these phenomena, as well as with risk incentive, investment incentive, and bankruptcy problems. The fixed nature of the debt claim, in conjunction with limited liability, is the prime source for the risk incentive, investment incentive, and bankruptcy problems.

3.31 Excessive Perquisite Consumption

Suppose you as owner-manager seek external equity financing while retaining complete control of the firm. You behave so as to maximize your utility from (1) money wages (which are assumed to be fixed), (2) the market value of your firm, and (3) on-the-job perquisites (which

---

[5] This section draws heavily from A. Barnea, R. Haugen, and L. Senbet, "Market Imperfections, Agency Problems, and Capital Structure: A Review," *Financial Management* (Summer 1981). The initial work on the financial theory of agency is largely due to M. Jensen and W. Meckling, "Theory of the Firm: Managerial Behavior, Agency Costs and Capital Structure," *Journal of Financial Economics* (October 1976).

are assumed to be *inseparable* from the firm).[6] *As sole owner,* you fully
bear the cost associated with additional perquisite consumption, and
you seek a utility maximizing combination of the rewards described
above. This balance is upset, however, once you sell a fraction of your
common shares to outsiders. In this case, you continue to enjoy the
full benefit of additional perquisite consumption, but you bear only
your proportional ownership fraction of the associated reduction in
the value of the firm's stock.

This is more clearly demonstrated in Figure 3.2. The trade-off
between the value of the firm and the (perceived) value of the perk
consumption is presented by the solid 45° budget constraint AB. For
a sole owner, the optimal combination of value of the firm and value

Figure 3.2. The Perk Incentive Problem

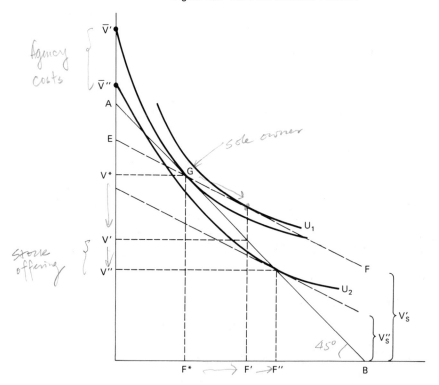

---

[6] A good example of a "perk" of this type would be expanding your span of control
beyond the level that would maximize firm value. You might value the social prestige
and power accompanying your position as chief executive officer and might be hesitant
to delegate authority, even when it would increase the market value of the firm to do
so.

of perk consumption is given by the tangency point G (V*, F*) where the highest possible indifference curve (U$_1$) is tangent to the budget constraint AB. Partial ownership changes the slope of the budget constraint, which represents the cost to the owner (in terms of reduction in the value of the firm) of $1.00 of perk consumption. Suppose, for example, you as entrepreneur seek to raise an amount of capital equal to V$'_S$ in Figure 3.2 by selling 50 percent of the shares of stock in the firm to outsiders. Your trade-off between wealth and perk consumption now shifts to the dotted line EF. Note that you now pay only $.50 (in terms of loss of your wealth) for each $1.00 in additional perks you consume. As a *partial* owner, you maximize your utility by increasing your perk consumption to F', reducing the value of the firm to V'.

With rational expectations, outsiders are aware of your incentive to increase "perk" consumption. They make unbiased estimates of the costs associated with the increased perk consumption, and they pass these costs back to you in full, in the form of a commensurate reduction in the price they are willing to pay for the securities you initially desire to sell. Thus, if outside stockholders are rational, they will offer only 50% of V''' = V$''_S$ for the stock. Note that the dollar equivalent of your utility as sole owner (with V*, F*) is $\overline{V}'$, while your dollar equivalent utility as partial owner (with V'', F'') is $\overline{V}''$. The difference ($\overline{V}' - \overline{V}''$) is the agency cost associated with raising capital V$''_S$ through a stock offering.

As more outside capital is required to finance the firm, the loss of value due to excessive perk consumption becomes larger. In essence, it appears that you, as the manager, are left with a combination of benefits in the form of dollar wealth and perquisites that is undesirable relative to your optimal combination as sole owner. Thus, in attempting to finance the firm through sale of common stock, you suffer a welfare loss that may be described as an agency cost.[7]

3.32 The Incentive of Stockholders to Bear Unwarranted Risk

The fact that stockholders may benefit by investing in high-risk projects is best demonstrated by considering equity as a European-type call option to buy back the entire firm from the debtholders at maturity, at an exercise price equal to the principal amount of the debt. The debtholders can be viewed as buying the assets of the firm

---

[7] A similar problem occurs if the owner-manager seeks financing through debt securities. Given limited liability, if the probability of default on the debt increases with increased perk consumption, the manager bears only a (decreasing) fraction of the associated cost. Again, however, assuming rationality, that portion of the costs not borne directly will be incurred, when the securities are issued, in the form of lowered proceeds of sale.

and issuing the call option (equity) on these assets. It is easy to understand this if the debt is in the form of pure discount bonds so that
the time of expiration of the option (equity) is the maturity date of
the bonds. Since (in the framework of the option pricing model of
Black and Scholes) the value of this call option increases with the
variance of the cash flows of the underlying assets, stockholders will
increase the market value of equity, at the expense of debtholders,
by selecting high-risk projects. For expositional purposes, suppose
that two projects, A and B, with differing risks, are available to the
firm. If both low- and high-risk projects available to the firm have
the same market value, the choice does not affect the total value of
the firm. It affects only the distribution of the value between bondholders and stockholders. Rational bondholders recognize the investment alternatives and stockholder risk incentives. Thus, they offer
a price for the debt that reflects the distribution of wealth given
adoption of the high-variance project. In any case, since both projects
command the same value, no cost is incurred by either party.

The situation is more serious, however, if the high-variance project
commands a lower market value. This situation is depicted in Figure
3.3, where the total value of the firm (project) is plotted on the horizontal axis and this value is split into debt and equity on the vertical
axis. The solid curve, labeled A, gives the relationship between stock
value and project value given that the project's variance is equal to
that of project A. The broken curve, labeled B, shows the same relationship given that the project has the higher variance of B. Note
that if stockholders have a choice between projects A and B, they will
choose B, even though it has a lower total value, since $V_S(B) > V_S(A)$.

Figure 3.3. The Risk Incentive Problem

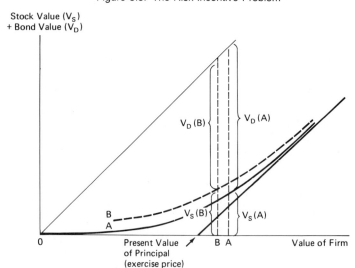

Given the principal amount of the debt (the exercise price), the price of debt is $V_D(A)$ if priced in accordance with the adoption of the superior (but low-risk) project, but it is $V_D(B)$ if priced with the presumption that the inferior (but high-risk) project is adopted. If bondholders have no means of neutralizing the stockholder incentive for risk shifting, they would presume that the inferior (but higher-risk) project will be adopted, and hence offer a price of $V_D(B)$. Unlike the previous case, the price reflects not only the higher risk, from which equity holders benefit, but also the inferiority of the project in terms of current value. If stockholders wish to finance the superior project, they will lose, since the bond price will go up to $V_D(A)$ from $V_D(B)$, and commensurately the stock price will decline from $V_S(B)$ to $V_S(A)$. Thus, they are forced to adopt the inferior project with the smaller value. This differential in value is an agency cost, which, on the surface, appears to be borne by stockholders.

3.33 The Incentive of Stockholders to Forgo Profitable Investments

Following Stewart Myers,[8] this case considers a firm that now (time 0) holds an option to invest in a given project at a future date (time 1). Based on those opportunities, the firm issues (at time 0) debt with a face value of D, which matures (at time 2) *after* the true market value of the investments is revealed (at time 1). This debt is *entirely supported by the current value of the future investment opportunity.* At time 1 the firm faces a decision whether to exercise the option (i.e., undertake the investment). At time 1 some state of nature, S, will exist that will be consistent with some market value of the investment opportunity. In the absence of debt financing, the firm accepts any investment for which the market value net of the required dollar investment is positive. That is, if the present value of expected future cash flows from the project exceeds the required investment, I, the investment will be made. But given the outstanding debt, stockholders maximize their wealth by accepting an investment only if its market value exceeds the debt obligation. Otherwise, it is in their best interest to default. This is illustrated in Figure 3.4. We have ordered time 1 states of the world (plotted horizontally as S) based on the associated market value, $V(S)$, of the projects. In the figure, project values increase in a simple linear fashion as we move from one state to the next, but this obviously need not be the case. An all-equity firm will make the investment in every state where the revealed market value of the project is greater than I. Thus, the project is adopted in

---

[8] S. Myers, "Determinants of Corporate Borrowing," *Journal of Financial Economics* (November 1977).

Figure 3.4. The Investment Incentive Problem

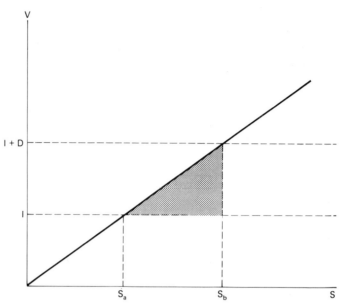

every state to the right of S_a. However, if the firm has debt outstanding that has a time 2 claim, the time 1 value of which is D, it is in the interests of the stockholders of the firm to reject the project and then default on the claim at time 2 in all states where the time 1 market value of the project is revealed to be less than I + D. Thus, the levered firm defaults in all states up to and including S_b.

In this situation, the value of the unlevered firm is given by

$$V_U = \int_{S_a}^{\infty} q(S)[V(S) - I]d_S$$

and the value of the levered firm by

$$V_L = V_D + V_S = \int_{S_b}^{\infty} q(S)D \, d_S + \int_{S_b}^{\infty} q(S)[V(S) - I - D]d_S$$

Note that those state values represented by the shaded triangle are lost, since the stockholders will not adopt the project in these states and the bondholders cannot exercise their claim until time 2. Thus $V_U > V_L$. Obviously, rational bondholders recognize the increased probability of default on their claims and discount it in the price they are willing to offer the firm for its bonds, V_D. Consequently, the stockholders, once again, are apparently forced to suffer the full burden of this agency cost.

Refer to Millers 77 (this book)
Bondholders bear the agency costs of get the benefits

"Assets in place"

Suboptimal future investments can also occur when the currently outstanding debt is issued against the currently held assets. This is unlike the previous case in which debt is entirely supported by future investments. Stockholders, however, cannot capture the full benefits of future investment opportunities, because they partially accrue to bondholders in the form of a reduction in the probability of default. Consequently, investment incentives may be curtailed despite the possibility that these opportunities generate a positive net present value for the firm as a whole. As before, equityholders suffer the full burden of the associated agency cost, because bondholders are unwilling to pay for future benefits due to the moral hazard problem.

3.34 Bankruptcy Problems

It is well known that if the transfer of ownership from stockholders to bondholders under default is costless, the mere possibility of bankruptcy should have no impact on the capital structure decision. However, since it is impossible to write contracts that specify clearly and unambiguously the rights of claimholders under all contingencies, one or more of the parties may precipitate a dispute that may be resolved in the process of formal bankruptcy proceedings. These proceedings are not costless; they involve a legal process which itself consumes a portion of the remaining value of the firm's assets. Moreover, the formal process of transferring ownership may disrupt the normal activities of the firm, precipitating a deterioration in long-standing customer and supplier relationships.

As significant as the costs associated with formal bankruptcy proceedings may be, they should not be confused with the costs associated with *liquidating* the firm's assets (the issue of bankruptcy cost significance is addressed in Chapter 5).[9] Bankruptcy and liquidation are best considered as distinct and independent events. Neither event is necessarily sufficient to trigger the other. The firm liquidates if and only if the market value of the firm as a going concern falls below its dismantled value under liquidation. Many authors have attributed the costs associated with distress sale of the assets of the firm to the event of bankruptcy. This is inappropriate, because while the proportion of debt in the capital structure affects the probability of bankruptcy, in no way does it affect the probability of liquidation. Liquidation is, in a complete sense, a mere capital budgeting decision. There is no *necessary* link between the decision to liquidate and the ability to pay off debt claims. A firm on the brink of bankruptcy should be liquidated only if the value of its assets as a going concern, net of the reorganization costs, is below the dismantled value under liquidation.

---

[9] See also R. Haugen and L. Senbet, "The Insignificance of Bankruptcy Costs to the Theory of Optimal Capital Structure," *Journal of Finance* (May 1978).

By the same token, a nonbankrupt firm that fits this same test must be liquidated. At any rate, the expected value of bankruptcy costs, if any, can be said to be borne by equityholders if debt is sold to rational investors. Thus, bankruptcy problems are identical to other agency problems with respect to cost incidence.

3.35 The Agency Problem of Informational Asymmetry

Consider a management that seeks to finance a project by selling securities, while the true nature of the return distribution of the project is unknown to the outside market. Management possesses valuable information about the project that is unavailable to the market. If this information were revealed to the market without ambiguity, the market would value the project at V_A. Otherwise, the market is unable to distinguish this project from another *less* profitable project with a value of V_B. This is a problem of informational asymmetry. It does not imply that management has better, or more, information than the market, but that it possesses some information that is valuable but unavailable to the market without which the market cannot identify the true nature of the project before it is undertaken.

This asymmetry may be resolved, at a cost, through various "signaling mechanisms." In the absence of an unambiguous signal, however, management will obtain less for securities sold than their "fair value" reflected in the true nature of project A. The difference between the "fair" price and the actual price is the agency cost associated with informational asymmetry, and it exists for the issuance of debt as well as new equity securities, provided that there is a differential probability of bankruptcy for the two projects.

It should perhaps be noted here that this particular agency problem is unique, because unlike the others, it cannot be resolved costlessly through arbitrage in the financial markets. (See Chapter 5.) Consequently, this problem may be more significant than the others in terms of inducing yield differentials between securities and optimal capital structure. We wish to emphasize that a going concern faces a continuing problem of informational asymmetry. The problem is not merely one of identifying the nature of new projects, but also one of identifying the nature of the current distribution of returns to the entire firm whenever additional financing is needed.

3.4 Consistency Between the Economic and Financial Agency Theories

3.41 Efforts, Perquisites, and Project Selection

It is clear that what economists call "effort" is analogous to perquisites (perk) consumption and selection of projects or investment decisions in the financial literature. Consumption of perks by agents reduces the value of the firm in the same way as negative (reduction) investment in efforts. Selection of high-risk and low-value projects and the loss of investment opportunities by agents have the same implications on the value of the firm as reduction in efforts.

Jensen and Meckling, who first elaborated the financial theory of agency, did not focus on possible solutions of the incentive problems associated with perk consumption, but rather on the costs involved with any exogenously determined level of external capital needed to finance the firm and the associated partial ownership. There is, however, an *implicit* constraint that the fractional ownership interest must be sufficient to preserve managerial control. Note that in the economic models the level of partial ownership is endogenous, in that the distribution of output is determined by the employment contract. Jensen and Meckling (see footnote 5) recognize that "the establishment of incentive compensation systems which serve to more closely identify the manager's interests with those of the outside equityholders . . . (have the) potential for controlling the behavior of the owner-manager" (p. 323). But they do not develop the framework in which Pareto-optimal incentive contracts are derived and optimal monitoring mechanisms are structured.

It is well understood by all financial writers that if perfect and costless monitoring is available, agency problems associated with motivation are easily resolved. Also, it is quite clear that if perfect monitoring (full information) is available, the risk incentive and the forgone investment opportunity problems can be resolved by contractual arrangements that promise particular sets of projects (returns). There is no moral hazard in this promise if it is backed by penalties that are collateralized by personal wealth.

Problems do emerge, however, when perfect monitoring is not available or when it is costly to implement. Financial writers encounter this problem by offering complex contractual arrangements that are based on marketable securities issued by the agent or on bond covenants (see Chapter 6). The prevailing financial theory of agency does not endogenize the form of such contracts, but it evaluates the efficacy of exogenously specified contractual forms in resolving various classes of agency problems.

3.42 Unlimited Versus Limited Liability Contracts

There is no explicit consideration of the risk sharing problem by financial writers. Recall that this is a central issue in the economic theory of agency. On the other hand, they deal with risky debt—an immediate consequence of limited liability. Therefore, the simple first best solution to the incentive problem prescribed by the economic theory of agency under risk neutrality—the issuance of risk-free debt—is not admissible. The focus on risky debt is due to an appeal to realism because of the dominance of limited liability in financial contracting, but it is not endogenously developed as an efficient means to raise capital.[10] Risky debt implies some degree of risk sharing by stockholders (agents) and bondholders (principals) but the financial literature does not claim nor doubt the optimality of this risk sharing solution. The omission of risk sharing considerations is well explained by noting that the firm is assumed to be a small fraction of the capital market. Stock- and bondholders hold diversified portfolios and value maximization is taken as the sole objective of the firm. The issue of utility maximization for nondiversified managers is circumvented by assumptions regarding the operation of markets for managerial skills (see Chapter 5).

3.5 Conclusion

The economic theory of agency focuses on contractual arrangements that provide an incentive to agents to invest the appropriate amount of efforts required by the objectives of principals. Such arrangements are called "first best" when they also produce an optimal sharing of the risk of the venture. If either the principal or the agent is risk averse, or if information is limited (i.e., when the amount of effort or the state of the world are not independently observable), first best contracts are not attainable. Second best contracts that utilize proxies for the missing information are suggested. Improvements in those contracts are possible once innovation in structure or more detailed and reliable information become available at reasonable costs.

Agency problems in finance are commonly in reference to external financing characterized by limited liability provisions. It has been shown that agents acting in their own self-interest will generally consume more perks, engage in high-risk (low-value) projects, forgo profitable investments, and increase the expected costs associated with bankruptcy. The costs that emerge as the result of such policies are borne by agents, as rational financiers foresee the costs and price them into the value of the securities purchased. The next chapter examines the role of such agency problems in generating optimal financial behavior by firms.

---

[10] The existence of limited liability provisions in prevailing financial contracts may be viewed as a natural consequence of contracting under a risk averse environment, because it is a means of risk sharing. Under the tradition of the fixed pay-off to the principal (i.e., unlimited liability to the agent), the risk neutral agent bears all the risk. When we go from risk neutrality to risk aversion, we naturally move from unlimited liability to limited liability. The challenge in financial contracting is to design financial packages that preserve limited liability provisions while resolving agency problems. In the presence of well-functioning financial markets, this seems feasible, as we shall see in later chapters.

Agency Costs and an Optimal Capital Structure

4.1 Introduction

IN Chapter 3 we discussed the nature of the various agency costs associated with issuing debt and equity capital. The costs arise because of conflicts of interest among financial claimholders. There is a conflict associated with equity capital between the owner-manager (or existing shareholders) and external (or new) shareholders. Debt capital causes conflict between stockholders and bondholders. Outside stockholders are concerned with the consumption of on the job per quisites by the owner-manager, and bondholders are concerned with the expropriation of their wealth by stockholders who may take unwarranted risks, forgo profitable investment opportunities, or precipitate disputes in bankruptcy proceedings. These conflicts may become more pronounced as the firm attempts to raise additional amounts of capital through a particular source, debt or equity. Consequently, it is possible that the firm may be able to minimize the costs associated with external financing by carefully balancing the relative amounts of equity and debt in its financing strategy.

In addition, as we saw in Chapter 2, debt financing has a desirable feature in the form of a tax subsidy, which may offset the costs associated with its agency problems. Thus, the firm may wish to issue an optimal amount of debt to avoid taxes even if agency costs of equity are insignificant. Interest payments on debt are deductible from income for purposes of computing the corporate income tax. In a sense, the firm receives a tax subsidy from the government when it issues debt capital. As a consequence, an optimal level of debt financing may still be achieved by issuing units of debt until the agency cost is exactly equal to the tax benefit at the margin. Thus, an optimal debt-equity ratio may exist (either) as a result of trading off the relative agency costs associated with debt and equity (or) as a result of balancing the (tax) benefits and (agency) costs of debt capital alone.

This chapter abstracts from complex contracts and market mechanisms as possible solutions to agency problems. These are subjects of subsequent chapters, but here we consider two separate scenarios. The *first* assumes away taxes and considers a closely held firm that is controlled and managed by a single entrepreneur. For this firm, managerial perquisite (perk) consumption increases with the fraction of the firm's stock held by outsiders. The issuance of equity capital involves a cost that is traded off against the costs of debt capital pursuant to an optimal financing strategy. The *second* scenario introduces the corporate income tax and considers a firm that is publicly held. No single shareholder holds controlling interest. The manager of the firm holds an insignificant proportion of the shares outstanding. For this type of firm, perquisite consumption on the part of management may indeed be a problem, but the severity of the problem is unrelated to the issuance of additional amounts of equity capital to outsiders. The issuance of equity capital is costless in this sense.[1] While equity capital may be costless in this case, it does not dominate costly debt capital as a form of finance. This is true because debt has an associated benefit (the tax subsidy) as well as associated costs (agency problems). If, as additional units of debt are issued, benefits and costs would converge at the margin, resulting in an optimal level of debt financing for the firm.

We stress that, even in the presence of debt-equity related agency costs and tax benefits on debt, an *interior* optimal capital structure may not exist for all firms. That is, it may be optimal for some firms

---

[1] If a managerial penalty exists that is tied to bankruptcy, managers may be able to signal to the market their personal evaluation of the profitability of the firm through the amount of debt they are willing to issue. In this sense, if management knows the firm to be more profitable than the current market value of the shares, it may signal this fact by issuing debt. The market will realize that management would not risk incurring the bankruptcy penalty if it were not convinced that the firm were profitable. As a consequence, the firm's prospects are reevaluated and its market value increases (up to a point) with the amount of debt in its capital structure. Conversely, the value of the firm falls as debt is displaced by equity. This may be thought of as an additional cost of issuing equity capital, which is associated with information asymmetry between the firm and the market. For more discussion on this point, see S. Ross, "The Determination of Financial Structure: The Incentive-Signalling Approach," *The Bell Journal of Economics* (Spring 1977).

to adopt *corner solutions* for its financial policy, assuming either all equity or nearly 100 percent debt. The existence of an *interior optimum* depends on the nature of the functions relating tax benefits and agency costs to the amounts of capital issued. In the following sections, we pay particular attention to the conditions under which agency problems lead to the type of "interior" balance between debt and equity financing that appears to exist for most contemporary firms.

4.2 The Trade-Off Between Agency Costs of Debt and Equity Capital

1st Scenario

In this section, we focus on a closely held firm that is controlled and managed by a single entrepreneur. The manager seeks external financing either because he or she has insufficient resources to establish and run the firm alone, or because he or she is risk averse and wishes to invest funds elsewhere to obtain the benefits of portfolio diversification. In any case, agency-related costs are associated with issuing both debt and equity capital, and the entrepreneur chooses a financing strategy that minimizes the aggregate of these costs.

4.21 The Total and Marginal Agency Cost Functions

Before determining the optimal debt-equity mix, the entrepreneur first determines the optimal *scale* of financing, or the total amount of external funds to be obtained. If the entrepreneur has insufficient resources to establish the firm alone, the deficiency obviously provides a lower limit. However, the financing requirement may exceed this limit in order to allow the manager to access the benefits of risk diversification in financial markets. Raising additional capital, even in optimal debt-equity proportions, involves the incidence of additional agency costs. The entrepreneur raises additional units of capital until, for the last unit raised, the marginal benefit associated with diversification equals the marginal cost associated with agency problems. At this point, the optimal *scale* of external financing is reached. → MC=MR
Given a scale of financing, there exists an optimal fraction of the funds to be obtained through debt capital. At this fraction, the total agency costs associated with raising the given volume of funds are minimized. Figure 4.1A depicts the total agency costs associated with debt and equity financing as a function of the fraction that is obtained through the issuance of debt. The agency cost of debt is partitioned into the components associated with the risk, investment, and bankruptcy problems. The broken curve is simply the summation of the agency cost functions for both equity and debt capital. Figure 4.1B plots the absolute value of the first derivative of the equity agency cost curve and the first derivative of the debt cost curve. Note that as you move to the right on the horizontal axis, debt financing displaces equity financing, and as you move to the left, equity displaces debt.

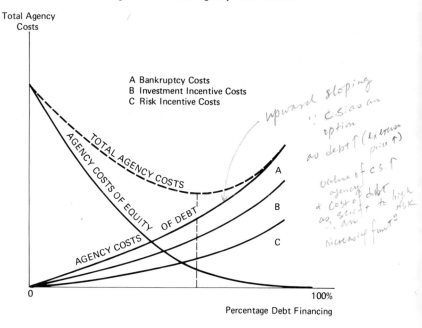

Figure 4.1A. Total Agency Cost Function

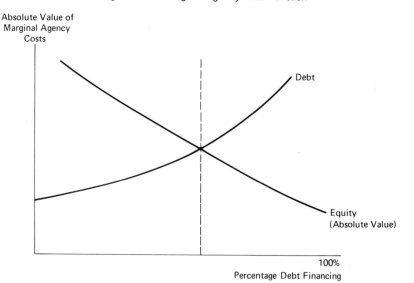

Figure 4.1B. Marginal Agency Cost Function

Figure 4.2.

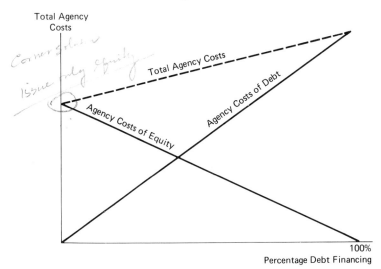

Thus, the marginal function for equity capital reflects the assumed condition that as additional units of *equity* are issued, each successive unit is accompanied by a higher incremental agency cost. The diagram, therefore, depicts a situation where the agency costs associated with both debt and equity are increasing at the margin. Note that total agency costs are minimized at the point where the marginal costs are equal. As drawn, this point provides the interior optimal ratio of debt to equity for the firm.

Such an *interior* optimum need not exist, however. Consider, for example, the total agency cost functions of Figures 4.2 and 4.3. In Figure 4.2, the marginal cost associated with issuing additional units of both debt and equity capital is presumed to be constant, and the marginal cost of equity is less than that of debt. In this situation, a corner solution exists. The firm minimizes total agency costs by issuing 100 percent equity capital to outsiders. A corner solution also exists in Figure 4.3. Here, agency costs are presumed to decline at the margin as additional units of debt and equity are issued. Given these specific functions, the firm now minimizes total agency costs by issuing 100 percent debt. Thus, a *rising* marginal agency cost function for either debt or equity capital is a necessary condition for an interior optimal financing strategy. In the next sections, we address the issue of whether it is reasonable to expect such a condition to exist as a general case.

Figure 4.3.

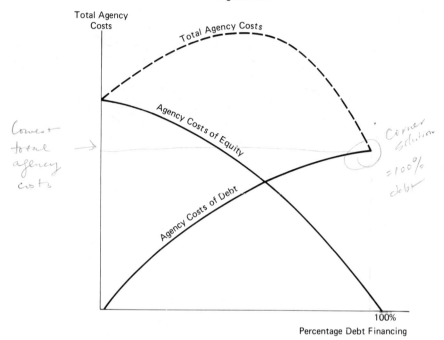

Percentage Debt Financing

4.22 The Marginal Agency Costs of Equity Capital

The solid 45° line in Figure 4.4 depicts the trade-off between firm value and perquisite consumption by the owner-manager. As sole owner, the entrepreneur maximizes utility (as represented by indifference curve U_0) by choosing the mix of perquisites (perks) and value given by \$70:\$30, respectively. Suppose that the manager seeks to raise additional capital by selling to outsiders a fraction α equal to 40 percent of the shares of the firm. Outsiders recognize that the cost to the manager of each additional dollar of perks consumed is now discounted to \$.60. The new trade-off between value and perks is given by line CD in Figure 4.4 which has a slope of $-(1-\alpha)$ or $-.60$. Outsiders recognize that it is optimal for the manager to shift perk consumption from \$70:\$30 to \$45:\$55 and will offer 40 percent of \$45 or an amount equal to \$18 for the stock. The entrepreneur shifts from indifference curve U_0 to U_1, which represents a dollar equivalent loss in utility of C_1. This is the agency cost associated with raising \$18 in external capital.

Suppose we slightly increase the amount of capital raised to \$21. The entrepreneur can raise \$21 by offering approximately 60 percent

Figure 4.4. Incremental Agency Costs with Incremental Equity Financing

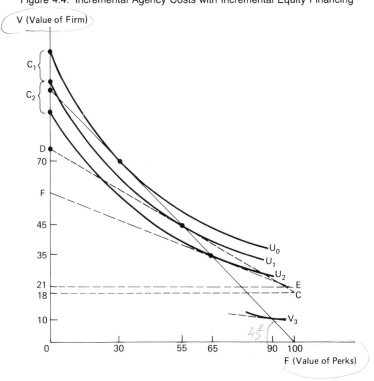

of the shares in the firm to outsiders. Outsiders recognize that, with perquisite consumption discounted to 40 cents on the dollar, the manager shifts to the mix of values and perks to $35:$65, and offers 60 percent of $35 for the shares, an amount equal to $21. Note, however, that the cost associated with raising the capital doubles, increasing by C_2. Thus, in the case depicted, agency costs associated with raising equity capital are, in fact, increasing at the margin.

Obviously, the nature of the marginal cost function is determined by the nature of the indifference curves (in the case depicted, the indifference curves are concentric circles centering at a common point). For example, curve U_2 might instead bend upward to intersect the vertical axis at a level that reflects a *declining* marginal agency cost. While such utility functions may be somewhat unusual, there are no persuasive arguments for excluding them from the feasible set. Nevertheless, the assumption of an upward sloping of the marginal agency cost function for equity capital at least does not appear to be unreasonable.

It is interesting to note that there is almost certainly a *limit* to the relative amount of equity capital that can be raised through external equity financing irrespective of what proportion of the shares are sold. For example, in the case of Figure 4.4 a smaller dollar amount of capital is raised by offering 90 percent of the stock to outsiders than is raised by offering 60 percent. This is because outsiders will anticipate perk consumption at $90 and offer only 90 percent of $10 for the stock. The relationship between the dollar amount of capital raised, V_s, and the fraction of the firm's stock sold, α, is given in Figure 4.5. This particular function is unique to the set of indifference curves depicted in Figure 4.4. However, the function should, as a general case, reach a maximum for $\alpha < 1$.

We now consider the agency cost functions for debt capital.[2]

4.23 Marginal Risk Incentive Costs of Debt

Recall that under the risk incentive problem the firm faces a choice of alternative investment opportunities with different variances of returns and market values. While the unlevered firm adopts the project with the highest net market value, the levered firm may find it in its interest to adopt a project with a lower net market value, if the variance of the project is sufficiently large. This is true because the common stock of the levered firm can be said to be priced as if it were a call option. The value of this option increases with the variance

Figure 4.5. Market Value of Stock Solid to Outsiders as a Function of the Fraction of Firm's Stock Sold

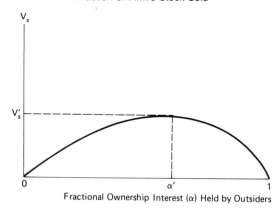

Fractional Ownership Interest (α) Held by Outsiders

---

[2] There exists another incentive problem, namely the agency problem of informational asymmetry, discussed in Chapter 3. This problem is endemic both to equity and debt capital. In discussing the principle of optimal finance, this chapter assumes away the incentive problem of informational asymmetry, but this is without loss of generality.

of the underlying asset (the project). For certain option pricing models, such as the option pricing model of Black and Scholes, the incentive to shift to higher variance projects is more pronounced the greater is the exercise price on the option (or the face value of the debt). This makes possible an increasing *marginal* agency cost function in connection with this particular problem. However, the existence of such a function depends on the nature of the set of investment strategies available to the firm.

Consider a firm that wishes to make a single investment. The firm has a limited degree of flexibility in choosing the production function associated with the investment. In choosing among alternative technologies, management changes both the risk and the market value of the firm (the project). Imagine that the firm's managers may select any position within the shaded region of Figure 4.6. If the firm is financed entirely with common stock, it is in the interest of managers to adopt the production function or technology that maximizes the total value of the firm (or in this case, equivalently, the common stock). Thus, managers would adopt the strategy given by point A, and the value of the firm would be $100. Suppose instead that the firm is financed in part with zero coupon bonds. We know now that if we

Figure 4.6. Agency Costs and Debt Financing Under the Risk Incentive Problem

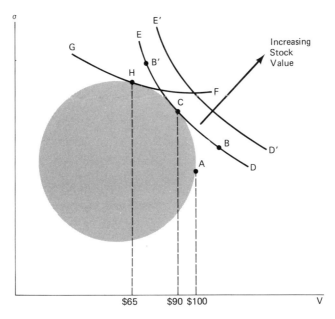

hold the market value of the firm's underlying assets constant but increase the variance of their returns, the market value of the common stock will increase. The market value of the common stock remains constant only if the market value of the underlying assets falls by a sufficient amount given the corresponding increase in their variance. As we move along curve DE we trade off asset value with variance in exactly this manner. At each point on the curve the market value of the common stock is a constant amount. For example, the market value of the common stock is the same at point B as it is at B'. While the value of the firm's *assets* is larger at B, the variance is smaller as well. The two effects cancel, giving the same stock (or option) value at B as at B'. Curve D'E' represents the same trade-off, but for a larger stock value. Management wants to attain a position on a curve representing the highest stock value possible. Given the firm's investment opportunity, this occurs at the point of tangency C. Strategy C results in a reduction in the total value of the firm from that which would obtain under all equity financing equal to $100 − $90 = $10. Since rational bondholders anticipate the adoption of the strategy in advance and discount it into the price they are willing to pay for the bonds, the $10 loss in value is imposed on the common stockholders as an agency cost.

Suppose now that the firm increases the amount of debt financing by increasing the face value of the debt. With a higher face value (equivalent to an exercise price if the common stock were a true option), a smaller increase in variance is sufficient to completely offset the effect of a reduction in the market value of the underlying asset on the market value of the common stock (the option). Thus, we are now dealing with a new family of curves, one of which is given by GHF in Figure 4.6. The stock value maximizing strategy is now at point H, and the associated agency cost is now given by $100 − $65 = $35. With the larger face value, the bonds will comprise a large percentage of the total value of the firm's assets. Note, however, that the value of the assets has declined from $90 to $65. Thus, in spite of the substantial associated increase in the agency cost ($25), the value of the additional debt capital raised may be very modest. As a consequence, in the case illustrated here, we have a rising marginal cost function for the risk incentive problem.

Given an assumed option pricing function for the common stock, it is easy to specify the families of curves associated with various face values of the debt. However, the magnitude of agency costs associated with various amounts of debt depend crucially on the nature of the shaded investment opportunity set. This, in turn, is likely to vary from firm to firm and, in fact, may take any arbitrary form. Given less than perfectly competitive conditions in the real sector of the economy, the investment opportunity frontier available to a particular firm may take a wide variety of shapes. Thus, with respect to this particular agency problem, we appear to be on less than solid ground in pre-suming the existence of an associated rising marginal cost function.

4.24 Marginal Investment Incentive Costs of Debt

The presence of debt financing may reduce management's incentive to commit capital to investment ventures that might otherwise be regarded as profitable, or which command a positive net present value. If the debt matures beyond the point in time when the option to execute the investment expires, the market value of the investment must exceed the sum of the required capital investment and the pre-sent value of the promised payment(s) to the bondholders. Otherwise, management will forgo the investment opportunity and default on the debt.

Recall the scenario relating to this problem that was discussed in Chapter 3. A firm has an option to make an investment of I dollars at the end of the first period at $t=1$. The investment opportunity has a positive net market value at $t=0$. At this time, the firm issues debt that is entirely backed by the market value of the investment oppor-tunity. The debt carries a single promised payment maturing at the end of the second period, or at $t=2$. A state of the world is revealed and its associated market value of the investment opportunity, $V_{(s)}$, is determined at $t=1$. The firm makes the investment commitment if $V_{(s)} > I + D$ where D is the value, at $t=1$, of payments promised to the bondholders at period 2. Note that, in the absence of debt fi-nancing, the commitment is made when $V_{(s)} > I$. Therefore, the debt reduces the number of states in which the investment is actually made.

This situation is depicted in Figure 4.7, where states of the world are ordered and plotted to create an increasing function for the mar-ket value of the investment opportunity. (State S_d is associated with the maximum value for the option.) As in Figure 3.4, the function is depicted as being linear, but this, again, need not be the case. Assume for the moment that state prices (the value at time 0 of a dollar to be received in state s at time 1) are uniform between S_a and S_d. In this case, market values at time 0 are proportional to *areas* within the diagram. For example, the market value of an all equity financed firm is represented by the area in the triangle ADE. On the other hand, if the firm issues debt, with promised payments having a present value of D at time 1, the market value of equity falls to the area within triangle GJE, while the market value of the debt is given by rectangle BDJG. The total market value of the entire firm falls by an amount proportional to the area in triangle ABG; this is the agency cost as-sociated with issuing the debt.

Now suppose that the firm doubles the (time 1) value of the prom-ised payments to bondholders. The investment is now made if and only if $V_{(s)} > I + 2D$. The market value of the new debt is CDHF

MYERS 1977

Figure 4.7. Marginal Costs and the Investment Incentive Problem

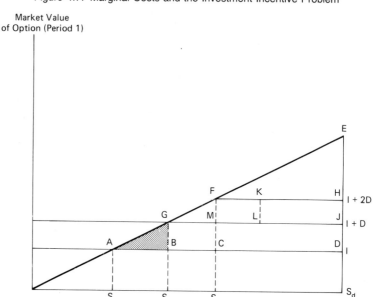

Period	0	1	2
	Debt Matures	State Revealed, Investment Made	Debt Issued

and the equity is FHE. Note that, if the area in BCMG is equal to that in MLKF, the marginal increase in the market value of the debt is LJHK while the marginal increase in agency costs is BCFG. Since we have a larger increment in costs associated with a smaller increment in the value of debt outstanding, we know that the marginal agency cost function is once again increasing for this case.

Whether we have increasing marginal costs for any given case depends on the nature of the market value-state function and the structure of state prices. Given the structure of state prices, concave functions are more favorable toward a rising marginal agency cost curve. Given the market value-state function, rising marginal agency costs are more likely if *higher* state prices are generally associated with higher market values of the investment option.

4.25 Marginal Bankruptcy Costs of Debt[3]

As we discussed in Chapter 3, formal bankruptcy proceedings may be associated with external drains of cash away from the firm. Cash may flow in the direction of lawyers, trustees, or accountants who execute the bankruptcy proceedings; to government, as a result of the loss of corporate tax shields, such as loss carryforwards; or to competing firms, as a result of any disruption that occurs in the relationships between the firm and suppliers and customers. Bondholders, at the time of the issuance of the debt, anticipate the possible incidence of these costs and discount their expected value into the price that they are willing to pay for the debt. Thus, the stockholders bear the burden of the costs.

As more debt is issued, the expected value of bankruptcy costs should increase, because the probability of bankruptcy and the incidence of the costs increases. In Figure 4.8A, costs incurred *at the time of bankruptcy*, C, are presumed to be known and independent of the magnitude of the bondholders claim, D, for a given firm. Assume also a one-period analysis where the terminal value of the firm $\tilde{V}_A$ roughly corresponds to a normal distribution, but with maximum value $V_A{}'$ and where investors are risk neutral. Under these conditions, the market value of the bankruptcy costs is given by $hC/(1 + r_F)$ where h is the probability of bankruptcy, E(C) is the expected bankruptcy cost, and r_F is the riskless interest rate. The market value of the bankruptcy cost as a function of the bondholders promised payment, D, is given by the solid curve labeled V_C in the lower portion of Figure 4.8A. The curve has the appearance of a cumulative normal distribution because as the amount of debt is increased, the terminal value of the firm sufficient to trigger bankruptcy increases and this terminal value is itself normally distributed. Thus as D increases, the probability of bankruptcy, h, increases as with a cumulative normal distribution. Curve V_D depicts the value of the debt as a function of the promised payment. As the probability of bankruptcy increases, the debt value approaches the discounted value of the assets of the firm, net of bankruptcy costs, from below.

The first derivatives of the debt value and bankruptcy cost functions are plotted on Figure 4.8B (since we are dealing with the first derivative, the marginal bankruptcy cost function is now in the form of a

---

[3] Again, recall that we are abstracting from market mechanisms to resolve agency problems associated with bankruptcy proceedings. See Chapter 5 for a discussion of such mechanisms. Our analysis of bankruptcy is intended to underscore the fact that there are complicating features, even if bankruptcy costs are assumed to be significant in absolute terms. That is, it is no longer readily apparent that a bankruptcy cost-tax subsidy trade-off leads to an optimal capital structure, as commonly argued in the traditional writing on this topic.

Figure 4.8A. Market Values of Debt and Bankruptcy Costs

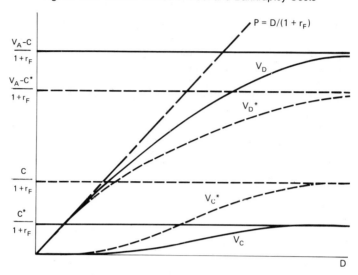

Figure 4.8B. First Derivatives of Market Values

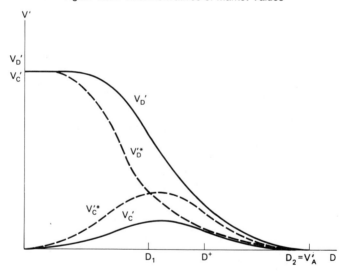

marginal normal distribution). Since both V_C and V_D change in response to a change in D, the change in V_C accompanying a change in V_D (the marginal agency cost function) can be inferred from Figure 4.8B. In the graph, as D increases, the change in V_C is assumed to continue to increase relative to the accompanying change in V_D. This means that the marginal bankruptcy cost function $\partial V_C/\partial V_D$ is continually rising (as the solid curve of Figure 4.9) with D and hence the amount of debt in the capital structure.

The marginal function can easily reach a maximum, however. This can easily be seen if we suppose that we increase bankruptcy costs to C* on Figure 4.8A. The debt value and bankruptcy cost value functions now approach lower and higher limits, respectively. The first derivatives of the curves may now intersect twice as they do in Figure 4.8B at D_1 and D_2 (the maximum possible value for the firm). The marginal bankruptcy cost function reaches a maximum at some point D^+ between the intersection points. Thus, for the broken curves of Figure 4.8B, the change in V_C* relative to the accompanying change in V_D* is maximized when the promised payment is D^+. Thus, in Figure 4.9, $\partial V_C/\partial V_D$ is maximized at debt level $V_D(D^+)$.

We should stress that an interior optimal debt ratio may still be consistent with a marginal bankruptcy cost function that reaches a maximum. Moreover, our analysis has assumed that the level of bankruptcy costs is unrelated to the magnitude of the bondholders claim. One might expect that at least the direct bankruptcy costs, such as

Figure 4.9. Marginal Bankruptcy Cost Functions for Different Levels of Bankruptcy Costs

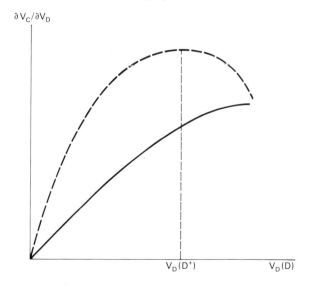

accounting and legal fees, are an increasing function of the amount of debt in the capital structure. This being the case, the chances for a continually rising marginal bankruptcy cost function are enhanced.

4.26 The Interior Optimum

We cannot guarantee that an increasing marginal agency cost function exists as a general case for all firms. A convincing case can be made for the argument that some firms may face a decreasing marginal agency cost function at least for debt capital. An interior optimal capital structure cannot exist for such firms unless they also face a decreasing marginal agency cost function for equity capital.

Figure 4.10 depicts a firm that faces an increasing marginal agency cost function for equity capital (recall that equity increases as we move toward the left on the horizontal axis) and a falling marginal cost function for debt capital. In this case, it is possible for the firm to attain an interior optimal capital structure. Suppose first that the marginal function for debt is given by the solid curve D and the equity function by the broken curve E. In this case, an interior optimal exists at A because marginal agency costs of debt and equity as a function of the leverage ratio are moving in opposite directions. As one moves to the left of A, the marginal cost of the next unit of equity is greater than the marginal cost of the unit of debt that it displaces. Therefore, it makes no sense to reduce the percentage of debt from that rep-

Figure 4.10. Marginal Agency Cost Curves

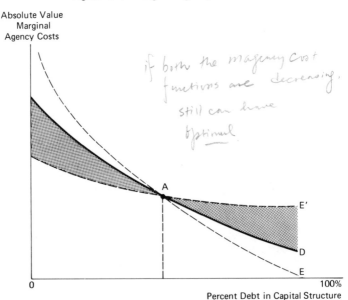

resented by point A. Similarly, as one moves to the right, the marginal cost of the next unit of debt exceeds the cost of the unit of equity that it displaces. Point A, therefore, represents the minimum cost position. However, if the equity function is given by broken curve E', we have a corner solution of all debt or all equity, depending on the relative size of the areas in the shaded portions of the graph to the left and to the right of A.

In Figure 4.11, the marginal function for debt rises and then falls. This may be the result of the fact that the firm is facing high levels of bankruptcy costs or it may be due to the shape of the firm's investment opportunity set relating to the risk incentive problem. In any case, a curve such as D opens the possibility of a corner solution, depending on the shape of the marginal function for equity. With function E we have an interior optimum at A, but function E' brings us to an all debt corner solution since the shaded area to the right of C exceeds that to the left. Note that, as the firm displaces equity with debt beyond point B, initially the costs associated with marginal units of debt exceed those of equity. However, as we move beyond point C, the cost differential reverses to an extent sufficient to make it profitable to adopt an all debt financing strategy.

Until this point, our discussion of the capital structure decision has related to trading off the costs associated with debt financing with the costs associated with equity financing. Equity costs stem from consumption, by the owner-manager, of on-the-job perquisites that may be said to increase as his or her fractional ownership in the firm decreases. While such a relationship may exist for the closely held

Figure 4.11. Marginal Agency Cost Curves

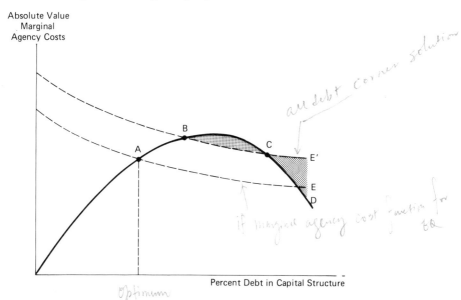

firm that is controlled by a single entrepreneur, costs associated with perk consumption are unlikely to be a significant factor in the *financing* of very large and widely held corporations. This is not to say that suboptimal consumption of perquisites by managers is not a problem for these firms, but it is a problem that is likely to be unrelated to the financing of a firm. Managers of giant corporations typically hold a trivial fraction, if any, of the total common stock outstanding. They are likely to be motivated more by the relationship between the profitability of the firm and the value of their own human capital than they are by the *fraction* of the firm's stock that is invested in their own personal portfolios. Thus, an increase in the fractional amount of stock held by outsiders is likely to have little effect on their behavior as managers. This being the case, the large firm can issue equity at little or no agency cost.

To the extent that debt capital has agency-related costs, equity would seem at first to dominate debt as a form of finance for the widely held firm. However, while debt may have associated costs, it also has a benefit in the form of the tax subsidy associated with the deductibility of interest payments. Thus, the large firm may achieve an optimal level of debt financing by trading off the tax benefits with the agency costs.

4.3 The Trade-Off Between Agency Costs and Tax Subsidy

In Chapter 2, we discussed the effect of the corporate income tax on the leverage irrelevance theorem of Modigliani and Miller. Since interest payments are tax deductible, the market value of the firm increases as additional debt is issued to displace equity. If the firm issues riskless perpetual debt, $V_D{}^+$, the value of the tax subsidy is $V_{\tau_C} = \tau_C V_D{}^+$ where τ_C is the corporate tax rate. The solid line in Figure 4.12 labeled $V_L = V_U + \tau_C V_D{}^+$ depicts the relationship between the value of the levered firm and the amount of perpetual debt issued.[4]

Obviously, in the absence of debt-related costs, any of the functions lead to a corner solution for the market value maximizing firm finance with nearly 100 percent debt. However, in the presence of debt-related agency costs, an interior optimal capital structure obtains when the present value of the expected tax savings is exactly offset at the margin by the present value of the expected agency costs. The curve labeled $C(V_D)$ in the lower portion of Figure 4.12 depicts the present value of expected agency costs as a function of the amount of perpetual debt issued. Note that the marginal agency cost functions are presumed to be positively sloped.

---

[4] The tax subsidy associated with issuing riskless, one-period debt, $V_D{}'$, is given by $T = \dfrac{\tau_C r^* V_D{}'}{(1 + r^*)}$, but if the debt is risky there exists a more complex, nonlinear function where both the first and second derivatives of this function are positive.

Figure 4.12. Trading Off the Tax Benefits and Costs of Debt Financing

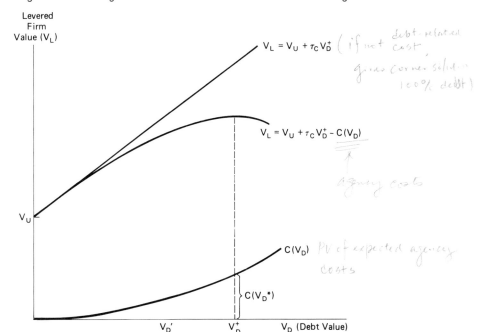

In the presence of debt-related costs, the value of the levered firm is given by the sum of its value as an unlevered firm and the present value of the tax subsidy, less the present value of expected agency costs.[5] The market values for the firm financing with perpetual debt are given by the concave function of Figure 4.12. The optimal debt level obtains at the maximum value for this function.[6]

The tax-cost trade-off results in an interior optimal capital structure regardless of the magnitude of the agency costs. This is true because, even if these costs are small, at some finite degree of leverage the present values of expected agency cost and the expected value of the tax subsidy may offset at the margin. However, if the preceding arguments are employed in order to reconcile existing financial theory with contemporary financial structures for observed firms, one must allege that the costs associated with agency problems are large unless one argues that bond yields are grossed up to reflect the tax advantage

---

[5] The incidence of bankruptcy costs may have an impact on the present value of the tax subsidy. Highly levered firms may go bankrupt even when profitable. In this case, corporate income taxes must be paid (by bondholders) in bankruptcy and bankruptcy costs may be considered a tax deductible expense. This interaction must be considered in computing the market value of the levered firm.

[6] Note that since $V\tau_C$ is convex to the origin V_L *may* not reach an interior maximum even if the agency cost function is increasing at the margin.

of debt to corporations. As discussed in Chapter 2, the supply curve for riskless perpetual debt is infinitely elastic at $r^*/(1 - \tau_C)$, under the Miller equilibrium, where r^* is the yield on securities that are tax exempt at the personal level. Firms will issue no debt at yields higher than $r^*/(1 - \tau_C)$, because at these yields issuing debt reduces the value of the firm. Conversely, they will issue debt in unlimited amounts at yields below $r^*/(1 - \tau_C)$, because debt increases the value of the firm at these yields. Given these supply adjustments, the equilibrium market interest rate on debt must be $r^*/(1 - \tau_C)$. At this rate, one *begins* from a position of indifference to debt *vis a vis* equity financing. This being the case, even expected agency costs that are small can have a significant impact on financing decisions and, as we shall see in Chapter 7, can result in an interior optimal debt-equity ratio in the observed range.

4.4 Conclusion

Agency problems may result in an interior optimal ratio of debt to equity financing in two distinct ways. *First,* if both equity and debt financing have related costs, the financier may issue units of debt and equity until the agency cost associated with marginal units is equal. This results in a minimization of the total cost associated with the financing effort if agency costs are increasing at the margin. This assumption appears to be reasonable for agency costs of equity capital. It is also reasonable for the bankruptcy and investment incentive costs associated with debt capital. However, there is no *a priori* reason to expect a rising marginal cost function to be associated with the risk incentive problem. It seems safe to conclude, though, that agency related costs may serve as a rationale for the financing decisions for many, if not all, firms.

For the large, widely held firm, excessive perquisite consumption by management is likely to be unrelated to the fraction of the firm held by outside stockholders. This means that equity can be issued without cost and the trade-off between equity and debt-related costs breaks down, assuming that informational asymmetry is no problem with new issuance of equity. If corporate taxes are introduced, however, the tax benefits of debt financing can be traded off against its costs to create an interior optimal capital structure.

Up to this point, we have abstracted from possible market mechanisms and the issuance of more complex financial instruments as possible solutions to agency problems. These mechanisms have material impact on the extent to which certain classes of agency problems are significant in optimal financial contracting. Chapters 5 and 6 deal with these important issues.

The Role of Markets in Resolving Agency Problems

5.1 Introduction

IN Chapter 2 we saw that if the environment is taxless and the capital market is functioning well, in the sense that traders eliminate obvious opportunities for quick profit, capital structure has no effect on the market value of the firm. If the market pays a premium for unlevered firms as opposed to levered firms, for example, it is in the interest of traders to capture the premium by buying both the bonds and stocks of levered firms as opposed to the stocks of other unlevered but otherwise identical firms. In other words, in the face of such a premium, portfolios of the bonds and stocks of levered firms, on average, have higher expected rates of return than portfolios of stocks of unlevered firms. As investors displace the low yielding portfolios of unlevered stocks with the higher yielding portfolios of bonds and stocks of levered firms, the market values of levered firms increase, and the premium in the market prices of unlevered firms decreases until it disappears completely. As a final result of this process, in equilibrium, the market value of any given firm is insensitive to changes in its capital structure. Conversely, if the levered firm sells at a premium, it pays to buy the stock of the unlevered firm and lever it on personal account. Again, the process of substituting personal leverage for corporate leverage leads to the disappearance of the leverage-related premium equilibrium.

The above argument relies on the assumption that the firm's investment strategy or the management of its assets can be taken to be independent of the nature of the contracts issued to finance its investment. In Chapter 4, however, we saw that conflicts of interest may exist between management and securityholders and among securityholders themselves. These conflicts may have a significant impact on asset management and investment strategy. Moreover, the magnitude of the costs associated with these conflicts can be related to the relative amounts of debt and equity in the firm's capital structure. In addition, as we shall see in Chapter 6, the magnitude of the costs can also be related to complexities in the contracts for financial claims. These complexities include, for example, those that relate to conversion and call privileges in corporate debt. In short, the assumption of independence between capital structure and asset management may be inaccurate.

In spite of this, one can still argue that markets are capable of costlessly resolving the conflicts of interest between the various parties of the firm, even if relationships between parties are delineated on the basis of very simple contracts. If these arguments are valid, the causal link between financial structure and asset management is broken, and we are once again back to the case of indifference to the form of finance. It must be said, however, that the forgoing arguments lean much harder on the efficient operation of the market than more traditional arbitrage arguments. Under the arbitrage argument stated above, for example, individual investors eliminate any capital structure related discounts or premia in the prices of securities as a result of the process of optimizing the composition of their portfolios. By avoiding securities selling at premia and constructing equivalent combinations of securities selling at discounted prices, investors, through their bids and offers, naturally eliminate both the premiums and the discounts. In contrast, the forgoing arguments require transactions that are larger in scale and more difficult to consummate. These transactions are associated with repurchase of the entirety of a given class of securities in the capital structure or, possibly, with the takeover of all classes of securities of the firm by outsiders. In addition, one of the two principal arguments detailed in this chapter relies on efficiency in the functioning of the labor market. In this market, conditions of perfect competition are less prevalent, transacting is more costly, and information flows less freely than in the financial markets. Consequently, because of (a) the nature of the transactions required in the financial markets and (b) the imperfections that exist in the labor markets, one might expect impediments to arise that would serve to block at least a complete resolution of agency problems through market mechanisms.

In sections 5.2 and 5.3 of this chapter, we discuss the roles of the financial and labor markets, respectively, in resolving agency problems. Our objective is to describe the potential means by which these markets resolve the conflicting interests between those parties associated with the firm. The concluding portion of each section is devoted to a discussion of potential impediments to the market mechanism that may stand as a barrier to a natural resolution of agency problems. As we shall see, to the extent that these barriers are significant, agency problems are significant to firm valuation and the determination of optimal capital structure.

5.2 The Capital Market

There are three distinct mechanisms by which agency conflicts can be costlessly neutralized through the capital market. The first involves (1) a uniting of the ownership interests of the firm's stockholders and debtholders. Interests are united when each of the stockholders (bondholders) buys a fraction of the bonds (stock) of the firm that corresponds to each of their fractional interests in the stock (bonds). In this sense, *financial unification* takes place individually among the firm's various securityholders. Financial unification is, thus, a phenomenon of collective ownership of *all* the outstanding securities irrespective of their form. A case in point is a simple separation property characterizing the capital asset pricing model where the market portfolio is collectively owned. In this case, incentive problems associated with security ownership no longer exist.

(2) The second mechanism, *informal reorganization*, is effective in limiting the costs associated with some types of agency problems, including formal reorganization or bankruptcy. If default is imminent, managers can avoid the associated costs by continually adjusting to an optimal capital structure, assuming there is one, and informally reorganizing the firm through issuing common stock and using the funds to repurchase the bonds of the firm at prevailing capital market prices. If existing management fails to informally reorganize the capital structure to an optimum, outsiders can take over the firm and then informally reorganize to capture an arbitrage profit. In this sense, management is disciplined to avoid agency costs through informal reorganization by corporate takeover. The third mechanism (3) involves the issuance of side securities called *contingent contracts* which, under certain conditions, serve to guarantee that the firm will follow a predetermined investment strategy that maximizes the total value of all its securities and thereby avoids agency costs.

5.21 Financial Unification

Agency problems can be resolved by uniting the ownership interests of the various claims on the firm's assets.[1] Consider, for example, the

---

[1] Unification of ownership rights was originally discussed by R. H. Coase in "The Problem of Social Cost," *Journal of Law and Economics* (October 1960), and by E. Fama in the context of financial markets in "The Effects of a Firm's Investment and Financing Decisions on the Welfare of its Security Holders," *American Economic Review* (June 1978).

incentive to increase the risk associated with the firm's assets and hence decrease the market value of outstanding debt while increasing the wealth of existing stockholders. Suppose the firm in question faces two mutually exclusive investment alternatives A and B. Alternative A has high risk but relatively low value, while B has low risk but relatively high value. Obviously, if the firm is financed with common stock alone, it is in the interests of stockholders to adopt investment B. This may not be true, however, for a levered firm. Suppose that the firm's total value is $10 if the low risk project is undertaken, and that given the bond contract this value is distributed equally between stockholders and bondholders. Recall also that the stock of the firm is conceptually equivalent to a call option to buy the entire firm back from the bondholders at maturity at an exercise price equal to the face value of the debt, assuming a pure discount bond (for a coupon bond, each coupon can be viewed as a pure discount bond). As such, the value of the stock (the option) is directly related to the variance of the returns to the firm's underlying assets. In fact, as we know from Chapter 3, the value of the stock may actually increase if the firm shifts to an investment strategy with a higher variance, even though the strategy implies a lower total market value for the firm's assets. Suppose that this situation prevails for the above firm, and if high-risk project A is undertaken, the stock value rises to $6 and the bond value falls to $3, leaving the total value of the firm at $9.

Management, acting in the interests of its common stockholders, announces that project A will be undertaken and the value of the firm falls to 9. Bondholders and stockholders can now capture a "pure" profit of 1 by uniting ownership interests in the firm and forcing management to change its strategy so as to maximize the firm's total value at 10. To illustrate, rational bondholders acquire proportionate interests in the stock of the firm that correspond to their proportionate interests in the bonds. (If they own 1/3 of the debt they will acquire a 1/3 interest in the stock.) In the same way, rational stockholders engage in similar acquisitions going the other way. Once the process is complete, there is no longer a conflict of interest between stockholders and bondholders, because their ownership interests are united. Under the existing tax code, the tax subsidy associated with the interest deduction is preserved under complete financial unification so long as the firm is not closely held.

In this sense, financial unification disciplines management to operate in the best interests of all securityholders by undertaking projects that maximize total firm value and not merely the value of the common stock. If the market is perfectly proficient in terms of the financial unification process, misallocation of resources and the associated costs of incentive problems can never occur. Obviously, under these circumstances, the expected value of these costs is zero and they will in no way affect the relative market values of the securities offered by the firm. Consequently, management will face the form of finance with indifference.[2]

5.22 Informal Reorganization and Takeover

If an agency problem associated with a bondholder-stockholder conflict is triggered by an event that occurs at a discrete point in time that can be accurately forecasted in advance, the cost associated with the problem can be avoided by adjusting the ratio of debt to equity to an optimum just prior to the occurrence of the event. If the cost associated with the event is significant, when the event becomes imminent, rational management will retire the debt by issuing stock to finance a repurchase at prevailing capital market prices. Subsequent to the occurrence of the event the debt can be reissued, again at prevailing capital market prices, and the proceeds can be used to repurchase the common stock previously issued.

The exercise of an option to make an investment is an example of one agency problem of this type. If the option must be exercised at a particular point in time, and if the presence of debt in the capital structure reduces the number of states in which the option will be exercised, then the optimal capital structure at the required time of exercise is 100 percent equity capital. If bondholders can be assured that the debt equity ratio will be continually adjusted to an optimum in this sense, the expected value of this type of agency cost is zero, as is its impact on the value of the debt securities and the total value of the firm.

Default on an interest payment is another example of an event that can be forecasted with accuracy, at least over relatively short time intervals. Suppose that such a default is imminent and will result in formal bankruptcy proceedings through the court system and the incidence of associated costs. Assume that the bondholder's fixed claim is $10, the market value of the total assets of the firm is $8, and the expected value of the bankruptcy cost is $2. The market value of the debt and equity adjust to reflect the expected incidence of the bankruptcy cost and the expected division of the wealth of the firm under formal reorganization. Assume that prices settle to $1 and $5 for the stock and the bonds, respectively. Acting on behalf of the stockholders, management should raise $5 in new capital by selling common stock,

---

[2] It is easy to see that the unification process is just as effective in resolving the problem of forgoing profitable investment opportunities in the presence of debt financing. Suppose a state of nature materializes whereby the market value of the project, V, is less than the discounted face value of the debt, but greater than the required investment commitment. It is then in the interests of bondholders to acquire the stock at its prevailing market value (presumably zero) and undertake the investment. In this case, the investment will be undertaken for all states where $V > I$ and the agency cost associated with the conflict is zero.

and use the proceeds to retire the bonds through repurchase. The basis of the stock sale is the market value of the bond investment, or $5. Bankruptcy is avoided, and the recaptured bankruptcy cost of $2 accrues to the old common stockholders as a pure profit. Note that in this example, and in general, management must repurchase *all* the debt, and not just a fraction thereof, in order to capture the entirety of the bankruptcy costs for the stockholders. If, instead, it attempts to avoid bankruptcy by repurchasing, say, just over 60 percent of the debt (thus leaving a *claim* by the remaining bondholders of 40), the recaptured bankruptcy costs would accrue to the remaining bond-holders, because they have the right to demand a full and complete payment of their claim and the firm now has the resources to pay such a claim in full. This is easily seen if we recognize that management must issue new stock worth $3 to retire 60 percent of the bonds (now selling in the market at a price of $3). If management pays the claim of $4 for the remaining 40 percent of the bondholders, this leaves $4 for the old and new stockholders, which is split between them as $1 and $3, respectively. No one gains from the transaction except the bondholders who refrained from surrendering their bonds at pre-vailing market values.[3] (free-rider problem)

This, of course, raises the question whether bondholders will be willing to sell at prices that reflect the expected division of wealth under formal reorganization. It is possible that they may only accept a tender offer at a price at which they share in some fraction of the recaptured bankruptcy costs. This is completely immaterial, however, *so long as the informal reorganization of the firm is consummated at some price* and the external drain of dollars away from the securityholders of the firm and into the hands of lawyers, competitors, etc., is avoided. Wealth redistribution between bondholders and stockholders that is incidental to informal reorganization can be anticipated *ex ante* at the time that the debt is issued. So long as these redistributions are *internal* to parties within the firm, they cannot in any way affect the total value of the firm. Thus, if securityholders can be assured that informal reorganization will always displace formal bankruptcy proceedings, the amount of debt in the capital structure will have no impact on the total value of the firm, at least not through the mechanism of expected bankruptcy costs.

Note also that if existing management fails to engage in informal reorganization, it is in the interests of outsiders to the firm to simul-

---

[3] Because of this, none of the bondholders may be willing to sell at prevailing market prices. This is an example of the free-rider problem discussed in Section 5.242 below. The problem may be overcome by imposing penalties on free riders in the bond indenture agreement. The economic consequences of such provisions should be anticipated by rational bondholders at the time of issuance. So long as their expectations are unbiased, the bonds will be priced objectively by the market with no loss to the firm.

taneously tender offers to both the bondholders and the stockholders of the firm. If the expected bankruptcy costs have been discounted into the prevailing market prices of these securities, outsiders can capture it through the takeover process.

5.23 Contingent Claim Securities[4]

Suppose that a deterministic relationship exists between the terminal values of firm A and firm B. The market values need not be identical, but if $V_{A,i}$ is the ith possible value for firm A, and $V_{B,i}$ corresponds in like manner to a firm B, which is in the same risk class, then the values for the two firms can always be related in the following way:

$$V_{A,i} = a_0 + a_1 V_{B,i} \qquad (5.1)$$

Note that the relationship is deterministic in the sense that the random movement in A is explained *entirely* by the movement in B with a coefficient of determination of 100 percent. A special case of this is the homogeneous risk class situation in which the terminal values differ only up to a scale factor with an identical expected return in equilibrium.

Assume that you are the manager of firm A. You know the nature of your firm (the probability distribution of its returns), your investment opportunities and strategy, and the fact that you will operate the firm so as to maximize its total market value. The problem is simply one of communicating these facts to the market in such a way that outsiders will believe that you are telling the truth. There are many other individuals ready to take advantage of any opportunity to deceive and expropriate wealth. Thus, if you are not absolutely convincing in your communication, the market assumes the worst and offers less than what you know to be a fair price for your securities.

Suppose you can identify another firm, B, the nature of which is known to the market, that happens to have the same investment opportunities, strategy, and quality of management as yours. Presume that this firm bears a relationship to yours, as given by the relationship of Equation (5.1). If this is the case, you can communicate the exact nature of the relationship between firms A and B and guarantee that you are telling the truth about your firm by issuing side securities, called contingent claims, which take the form of put and call options.

---

[4] Contingent contracts were originally discussed by A. M. Spence as a costless signalling device in "Competitive and Optimal Responses to Signals: An Analysis of Efficiency and Distribution," *Journal of Economic Theory* (March 1974). Contingent contracts taking the form of put and call options to *simultaneously* resolve agency and information asymmetry problems were discussed by R. Haugen and L. Senbet in "New Perspectives on Informational Asymmetry and Agency Relationships," *Journal of Financial and Quantitative Analysis* (November 1979).

These side securities can be distributed at the same time that you issue conventional securities to raise capital.

A conventional call option is a contract to buy an asset at a specific price (the exercise price) on or before a specific expiration date. A put option is similar except it gives the holder an opportunity to sell an asset at a specific price. Put and call options typically have exercise prices that are fixed at some amount. They need not, however. The exercise price, E, may be a random amount that is related in a predetermined fashion to some well-defined index such as, in our example, the future market value of firm B. Consider a call option contract to buy your firm that specifies an exercise price that is given by,

$$E_i = a_0 + a_1 V_{B, i} \qquad (5.2)$$

where the parameters a_0 and a_1 are identical to those in Equation (5.1). Given what you know about your firm, it is always true that $E_i = V_{A, i}$ and this call option has no value under all states of nature. Knowing this, you, as manager, can distribute large numbers of these call options, written on yourself, at no charge to the recipients. In doing so you exclude from possibility the following case,

$$V_{A, i} > a_0 + a_1 V_{B, i} \qquad (5.3)$$

because the possibility of such a case is inconsistent with rationality on your part. Similarly, you can also issue at no charge put options with identical exercise prices. These put options are also valueless in all states of nature. By issuing them, you communicate to the market that the following cases are also beyond the realm of possibility.

$$V_{A, i} < a_0 + a_1 V_{B, i} \qquad (5.4)$$

Thus, the joint issuance of the put and call options as side securities costlessly guarantees to the market the exact nature of your firm. Agency problems, including that of information asymmetry, are resolved without cost, and these problems can have no effect on either the firm's internal capital structure or its market value.

Obviously, it may be impossible for you to identify another firm with the required relationship to yours. If you cannot find a *single* firm that meets the requirement, it may be possible to specify in the option contracts (in terms of portfolio proportions) a *portfolio* of assets, the value of which corresponds in some deterministic way to the value of your firm. It is important to realize that your ability to construct such a portfolio is limited by the completeness of the capital market, in the sense of the number and variety of the investment opportunities that are available. If the capital market is complete, or if the market permits *complete spanning* of your firm by the existing assets, it is always possible to construct portfolios that produce specific desired returns that correspond to specific states of nature. In such a market, it is possible for all managers to specify portfolios whose values relate deterministically to all possible future values of what they know to be their firm. These managers can resolve all agency problems costlessly by issuing costless contingent claim securities. In this sense, we must conclude that agency problems can have an effect on the value of the firm only in the presence of *incomplete markets*, which do not allow complete spanning.

5.24 Impediments to Resolution by the Capital Market

In the previous section, a lack of market completeness or spanning was shown to be a barrier to a generalized costless resolution to agency problems through side securities. Similarly, other barriers may stand in the way of a costless resolution through financial unification, informal reorganization, and takeover.

5.241 The Free Rider Problem

A free rider is one who seeks a free lunch, so to speak. In the present setting, a free rider is defined as a stockholder or bondholder who attempts to capture a fraction of the profit that motivates a tender offer to buy the bonds or stock of a firm. Free riders decline the tender offer, but hope that a sufficient number of their fellow shareholders will accept and make the bid successful. If the bid is successful, the free riders, who remain, share proportionately in any increase in the value of the firm that results from the takeover. Because of this, it is in the interest of *all* shareholders to free ride,[5] so long as the bid price, P, is anything less than the expected value of their shares *subsequent* to a successful takeover, V_S. However, there is no motive to tender in the first place unless the shares can be exchanged at terms where $V_S > P$. This means that tender offers can never be successful unless something can be done about the free rider problem. Takeovers and informal reorganizations can never occur!

Takeovers *do* occur, however. They occur because shareholders impose penalties on free riders in the corporate bylaws.[6] These penalties serve to make the value of the acquired firm to a free rider different from its value to an acquirer. In essence, the penalties serve to transfer wealth from the free riders to the acquirers after the acquisition takes place. The penalties can take several forms. For example, the acquirers may be permitted by the bylaws to issue new

---

[5] The foregoing relies heavily on an analysis by S. Grossman and O. Hart, "Takeover Bids, the Free Rider Problem, and the Theory of the Corporation," *Bell Journal of Economics* (Spring 1980).

[6] Penalties on free riders can also be written in corporate bond indentures to facilitate the acquisition of debt on information reorganization.

shares to themselves. The bylaws may also allow acquirers to sell products produced by the firm to other firms already owned by the acquirers at discounted prices. In any case, the effect of such penalties is to increase the value of the firm to those who make the tender and reduce its value to those who free ride.

From the viewpoint of existing shareholders, an increase in the severity of the penalty can be said to have three effects. First, it reduces the price at which tender offers can be expected to take place. If the penalty is given by $\emptyset$, a rational bid price is max $(V_S - \emptyset, q)$, where q is the premerger price. Thus, as $\emptyset$ increases, the expected tender price decreases. Second, an increase in $\emptyset$ should increase the probability of tender offers when there are profits to be captured. (Recall that when $\emptyset = 0$ the probability of receiving a tender offer is zero.) Finally, since the threat of takeover disciplines management to adopt strategies that maximize the value of the firm, anything that enhances the probability of takover motivates existing management to strive toward efficient operation. Thus, while the first effect of an increase in $\emptyset$ is negative, the second two are positive.

Suppose there is perfect competition among those who bid for the firm. In this case, the competing bids will drive the tender price to $V_S - C$, as long as $\emptyset > C$, where C represents the cost to the bidder associated with making the tender. In the presence of bidder competition, increasing $\emptyset$ no longer reduces the expected tender price, but the attendant benefits are still present. Thus, if bidders actively compete, it is in the interests of existing stockholders to write bylaws imposing stiff penalties on free riders.

On the other hand, if less than perfect competition among bidders can be expected, shareholders must trade off the benefits and costs associated with imposing free rider penalties. If only a low level of competition can be expected, it is in the interest of shareholders to impose a low-level penalty on those who free ride. In this sense, the severity of the free rider problem in blocking informal reorganization or takeover is inversely related to the efficient operation of the financial markets. If the markets function well and there is a high degree of competition among raiders, the effect of the free rider problem is minimal.

5.242 The Value of Managerial Rights

Consider the problem of perquisite (perk) consumption by an entrepreneur who retains total control of the firm. This problem is discussed in Chapters 3 and 6. The situation depicted in Figure 5.1 is one where the entrepreneur has raised capital equal to V_S by selling roughly ⅔ of the stock of the firm to outsiders. The total market value of all the firm's shares is V' and the value (in terms of reduction in firm value due to inefficient operation) of perks consumed is F'. The market value of the entrepreneur's shares is $V' - V_S$.

Figure 5.1.

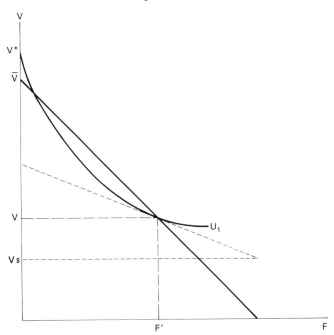

At first glance it seems that we can easily make a pure profit by taking over the firm. Why not offer $V' - V_s$ for the entrepreneur's shares and V_s for the remaining ⅔, manage the firm efficiently, and increase its value to $\overline{V}$, capturing a profit equal to $\overline{V} - V'$? We are precluded from doing this, however, because it is assumed that entrepreneurs, such as this one, retain total control of the firm,[7] and we can easily show that they will refuse to surrender their shares for their existing market value, which in this case is $V' - V_s$. This is because entrepreneurs who surrender their shares also surrender their managerial rights to consumption of on-the-job perquisites. In Figure 5.1 the utility associated with the combination of wealth V' plus perquisite F' is given by indifference curve U_1. The dollar equivalent of this utility level is V^*, and because of this the entrepreneur will decline any offer less than $V' - V_s$ to surrender control of the firm. Acceptable offers will, of course, not be forthcoming unless it happens to be true that $V^* < \overline{V}$. If $V^* > \overline{V}$, the capital market offers no solution to this particular agency problem.

---

[7] In the Jensen-Meckling analysis, the common shares issued to outsiders are presumed to be nonvoting.

5.243 THE LOCKED-IN EFFECT

Under the existing tax code investors pay taxes on capital gains only when they are realized and not as they accrue. That is, if you purchased an asset some time ago at a price below the prevailing price today, you need not pay taxes on the accrued capital gain until you actually sell the asset. Since postponing the sale of an asset also postpones the payment of the tax, the tax acts to reduce the supply of issues that have appreciated in price. In effect, by delaying sale, an investor who is in this way "locked in" receives an interest-free loan from the government equal to the amount of the tax liability. Because of this provision of the law, investors who are locked in may be unwilling to dispose of their shares at prices outsiders to the firm are willing to pay. They require a premium in the offer price in order to dispose of their shares. This, of course, increases the costs associated with takeover and informal reorganization in the real sense that, if those who are locked in surrender their shares, more dollars flow to the government than would otherwise be consistent with optimal tax planning. If insiders to the firm are rational, the cost associated with this additional drain of cash to the government must be paid by those acquiring the shares in the form of a premium in the offer price.[8]

The required premium may be significant. Consider a simplified case where investors are presumed to be risk neutral and have single period horizons. The firm pays no dividends, and capital gains are taxed at the rate τ_G. The expected value of the firm at the end of the period is $E(\tilde{V})$ and the rate of interest is r. The value of shares to an outsider to the firm is given by,

$$V_0 = \frac{E(\tilde{V}) - \tau_G(E(\tilde{V}) - V_0)}{(1 + r)} \qquad (5.5)$$

Solving for V_0 we get,

$$V_0 = \frac{E(\tilde{V})(1 - \tau_G)}{(1 + r - \tau_G)} \qquad (5.6)$$

Now consider an insider to the firm who originally acquired the shares at price V_I. The after tax proceeds to the insider for selling immediately at a bid price equal to P is

$$V_L = P - \tau_G(P - V_I) = P(1 - \tau_G) + \tau_G V_I \qquad (5.7)$$

---

[8] On the other hand, if capital gains taxes can be arbitraged at a *cost*, the premium reflects the *cost* of tax arbitrage rather than the nominal capital gains taxation.

On the other hand, the present value of the after tax proceeds to the insider of delaying sale until the end of the horizon is given by

$$V_H = \frac{E(\tilde{V}) - \tau_G(E(\tilde{V}) - V_I)}{(1 + r)} \tag{5.8}$$

The lowest bid price insiders will accept is one where they are indifferent between liquidating now or at their horizons. Setting (5.7) equal to (5.8) and solving for P we get

$$P = \frac{E(\tilde{V})}{(1 + r)} - \frac{\tau_G\, V_I\, r}{(1 + r)\, (1 - \tau_G)} \tag{5.9}$$

It is clear that the value of the stock to an outsider (Equation (5.6)) may differ from that to an insider (Equation (5.9)). For example, suppose the rate of interest is 20 percent, the tax rate is 50 percent, and the insider's original purchase price is $50. If the expected future value of the stock is $100, the insider finds a bid of $75 acceptable, but an outsider values the stock at approximately $71. The difference between the two values is a clear cost that the outsider must pay in order to gain control of the shares.

It is possible that any reluctance of insiders to sell can be overcome by imposing in the corporate bylaws penalties on minority stockholders similar to those discussed above under the free rider problem. The effect of such penalties, however, is merely to shift the costs associated with the locked-in effect away from those seeking control of the firm to those who must surrender their shares. The additional drain of dollars from shareholders to the government, in the form of higher taxes paid, still occurs. These costs can be anticipated in advance and their expected values can be discounted into offer prices made by new stockholders and bondholders at the time the firm originally seeks financing. The net result of the locked-in effect is a potential cost associated with avoiding agency problems through the capital market. To the extent that this cost is significant, or avoiding the taxes themselves is costly and impedes a natural, costless resolution, agency problems themselves become significant in valuing the firm and selecting the optimal form of finance.

Perhaps a more desirable method of avoiding the locked-in problem is through a tax-free exchange of securities. Rather than attempting to take over control of the firm through an offer of cash for securities, the "raider" may offer instead an exchange of securities, say an exchange of stock in the new firm for the old. In such an exchange, accrued capital gains on the old shares may be deemed to be unrealized from the viewpoint of the I.R.S. However, given that the returns on the new shares are distributed differently from the returns on the old, such an exchange may be accomplished by a cost associated with suboptimal diversification. Should the investor attempt to mitigate the cost by disposing of the newly acquired shares, the gains on the old shares will be deemed to have been realized and will be taxed accordingly.

5.244 CONTINUOUS INCENTIVE PROBLEMS

As discussed earlier, agency problems that are associated with discrete time events, such as default on a claim or opportunities to exercise options to invest in given projects, can be avoided through informal reorganization. If, for example, the investment option must be exercised at a particular point in time, costs associated with bond-holder-stockholder conflicts can be avoided by issuing stock and repurchasing debt an instant before the exercise date and reversing the transaction an instant thereafter.

However, consider the case of a continuous opportunity. Suppose a chemical firm is engaged in manufacturing some product. The product may be produced through either of two processes. The quality of the product produced under the first process is uniformly high. The cash flows anticipated from this process are also stable and relatively large. On the other hand, the second process produces a product of lower than average quality. In addition, the quality of the product and the anticipated cash flows under this process are more variable. Transferring the production function from one process to another is costless and *can take place at any time*.

If the firm is financed exclusively with common stock, it is clearly in the interests of the stockholders of this firm to adopt the stable process. This may not be true, however, if the firm has debt in its capital structure. Again, treating the stock as an option to buy the firm from the bondholders at maturity, the value of this option may be higher under the more variable process, even though the total value of all the firm's securities is lower. As noted earlier, this reduction in value is an agency cost associated with issuing debt.

There is also a tax benefit associated with issuing debt, however. The interest expense on debt can be deducted by the firm in computing taxable income. As we saw in Chapter 4, in optimizing capital structure, the firm trades off the agency cost of debt with its tax benefit until, at the margin, the cost and benefit associated with issuing the last unit of debt are equal. Optimizing in this way, the chemical firm may find the most desirable strategy to be one where it issues the appropriate amount of debt and then maximizes the value of its stock by adopting the more variable process. In other words, the agency cost is incurred in association with *optimizing* the debt-equity ratio and *maximizing* the total value of the firm.

Can transactions in the capital market prevent the incidence of this type of agency cost? Obviously, informal reorganization is no help, because the capital structure of the firm is already optimal. If the debt is repurchased, we eliminate the incentive to take risk, but the value of the firm actually falls, because we also lose the tax benefits of debt financing (over all the units of debt issued except the one at the margin, the tax benefit exceeds the agency cost). Nor can this cost be avoided through takeover of the firm by outsiders. A takeover bid is motivated by an opportunity to make a pure profit, but what profit is to be made here? The existing management has already maximized the total market value of the firm. If outsiders acquire the firm, it is in their interest to duplicate *the exact strategy* of the previous management with no gain in terms of market value. Obviously, a continuous incentive problem of this type cannot be neutralized by either informal reorganization or takeover.[9]

Continuous problems of this type *can* be neutralized through financial unification. If stockholders acquire proportionate interests in the debt of the firm and bondholders simultaneously follow a similar strategy, the conflict of interest disappears. Thus, the firm shifts to the stable process while preserving the tax shelters associated with debt financing. It should be noted, however, that this strategy involves a cost of its own. If capital markets are not complete, in the sense discussed above, splitting the ownership rights to the firm into debt and equity claims may create unique return distributions that are otherwise unavailable. By requiring investors to hold both debt and equity claims in their portfolios, they are in effect denied access to these unique distributions. Thus, they may suffer diversification costs as their portfolios deviate from desired, utility maximizing, investment proportions.

5.3 The Labor Market

In previous sections, we discussed the problem of the perquisite consumption incentive faced by entrepreneurs who seek external financing. As sole owners, the managers trade off the utility associated with shirking, incompetence, or on-the-job consumption of perquisites (perks), with their own loss of wealth associated with such misallocation of the resources of their firms. Since the managers, in this case, are presumed to be the sole owners of their firms, they pay in full for their consumption on the job; that is, they face a full "*ex post* settling up" for the perks they consume, with themselves as the securityholders. As *partial* owners, however, they no longer face a complete *ex post* settling up. Some of the costs associated with their perk consumption are borne by the outsiders from whom they raise capital. Thus, we

---

[9] The problem can be neutralized by writing complex provisions, such as conversion rights, into the bond contract. However, in this context, the form of the financial contract, and the nature of capital structure, become significant to the valuation of the firm.

have an incentive problem faced by entrepreneurs who seek outside financing.

In the original construction of the problem by Jensen and Meckling, the entrepreneurs' control over the firm is presumed to be absolute. Moreover, their wages are presumed to be fixed and unrelated to perceived performance. While this situation holds to a limited degree for some firms, it seems inappropriate in explaining managerial behavior in the large, widely held corporation.

In large corporations, managerial performance is monitored from several directions. Perhaps the ultimate internal monitor is the board of directors, whose role is to scrutinize decision making at the highest levels of authority. Monitoring also takes place by lower level managers who can reap rewards by stepping over shirking, or less competent, managers at higher levels. Since ongoing firms are always in the market for new managers, a third form of monitoring takes place outside the firm by other firms who scrutinize the performance of those who control their competitors.

Within this environment, managers pay, to a potentially large degree, for shirking or perquisite consumption, even if they own a very small proportion of the securities of the firm. They pay in the form of adjustment of their wages to the assessments of their performance by those who monitor them. As we shall see, if the market for managerial labor functions well, the present values of managers' future wages (their human capital) respond to changes in their perk consumption so as to impose on them a complete *ex post* settling up. That is, they pay in full for any perks consumed irrespective of the nature and relative magnitude of their ownership rights to the firm. In this environment, the incentive to consume perks is insensitive to the type of securities issued to raise new capital, and this particular agency problem is completely neutralized.

5.31 Conditions Required for Wage Adjustments to Impose a Complete *Ex Post* Settling Up

Suppose that the market for managerial labor is efficient in the sense that relevant information is freely available, and that the market is populated by rational participants who use information relating to the managers' current and past performances to formulate unbiased expectations relating to the managers' expected marginal services or products. Presume also that the wage of any given manager always quickly adjusts to this unbiased assessment of expected marginal product.

In any given period, the managers' actual marginal products may differ from what they contracted to deliver *ex ante*. Many of the deviations are likely to be attributable to chance factors that could not have been anticipated and have little to do with the managers' efforts and talents. Because of this, the managers' wages do not change in the next period by the full amounts of the observed deviations of actual from contracted marginal products. However, the following example shows that changes in the present value of their associated future wages can be as great as the cost to the firms of their deviations from contract.

Let the managers' measured marginal product for any one period be composed of (a) the expected marginal produce $E(Z)$ and (b) a noise term ε deriving either from events that cannot be anticipated or inaccuracy in measurement.

$$Z_t = E(Z_t) + \varepsilon_t \qquad (5.10)$$

if $E(Z_t)$ moves randomly over time it will evolve by the following process[10]

$$E(Z_t) = E(Z_{t-1}) + (1 - \phi) \varepsilon_{t-1} \qquad (5.11)$$

where ϕ is a parameter between zero and 1 and is larger the larger is the variance of the noise term in Equation (5.9). An equivalent expression to (5.11) is,[11]

$$E(Z_t) = (1 - \phi) Z_{t-1} + \phi(1 - \phi) Z_{t-2}$$
$$+ \phi^2(1 - \phi) Z_{t-3} + ... \qquad (5.12)$$

We can observe that if managers are paid according to (5.11) they do not avoid their *ex post* marginal product, even though they are paid, in each period, their *expected* marginal product. Consider the managers' marginal product in t, Z_t. It has a weight on the determination of next periods wage, $E(Z_{t+1})$, equal to $1 - \phi$, and a weight for the period thereafter equal to $\phi(1 - \phi)$ and so on. Over a perpetual stream of income, the impact on all future periods is exactly Z_t, assuming a zero interest rate. The marginal product in t is merely smoothed over the stream of future wages rather than being absorbed immediately as a change in the current wage. The smoothing or the weighting problem in (5.12) is endogenous in the labor market so as

---

[10] For a proof of this, see John Muth, "Optimal Properties of Exponentially Weighted Forecasts," *Journal of the American Statistical Association* (June 1960). This wage revision process is based on E. Fama, "Agency Problems and the Theory of the Firm," *Journal of Political Economy* (April 1980).

[11] An equivalent expression to (5.10) is

$$E(Z_t) = (1 - \phi) Z_{t-1} + \phi E(Z_{t-1})$$

so that the change in E(Z) from one period to the next is given by:

$$E(Z_t) - E(Z_{t-1}) = (1 - \phi)(Z_{t-1} - E(Z_{t-1})) = (1 - \phi) \varepsilon_{t-1}$$

to achieve appropriate diversification of undesirable variability of wages over time.[12]

If the labor market functions so as to set wages in this way, there is no need for complex managerial incentive contracts. Managers can merely negotiate to split their compensation optimally between dollar wages and on-the-job consumption. Since one form of compensation merely displaces the other, the market value of the firm is independent of the split. Moreover, consumption of perquisites is independent of the relative share and nature of the claims held by outside securityholders. Under an efficient labor market, if there is an optimal capital structure, it is unrelated to this particular form of agency problem.

5.32 Impediments to Resolution by the Labor Market

There are several reasons why the process described above may operate imperfectly. First, the market for human capital of this type is likely to be less efficient than the market for financial capital. Information needed to accurately assess performance flows less freely. Top level managers with the required technical skills to run firms in specialized industries may be limited in number, and the extent of competition for these positions may be less than perfect.[13]

In addition, for the very large firm, profits in the first few hours of operation may exceed the wages of even the highest level managers. This means that the variance of the noise term in equation (5.10) is likely to be very large. Recall that in the example the adjustment parameter Ø is directly related to this variance. Thus, for many firms it may take a very large number of future periods before current deviations between expected and realized marginal products are fully reflected in the managers' stream of future wages. For these firms, it may be in the best interests of rational managers to bury shirking or perquisite compensation in their *ex post* measured marginal products.

Top-level managers are also typically at an advanced stage of their working lives. This means that their earnings streams are likely to be truncated after a relatively few number of periods, too few perhaps

---

[12] This seems to hinge on the assumption that diversification through the capital market is more costly. Thus, the functioning of the capital market affects the design of a wage contract in the labor market. This is particularly important when we relax the assumption of zero interest rate in Fama's wage revision process through time. What is at stake in the wage revision process is not just smoothing but the impact of time itself through the term structure of interest rates.

[13] The relative efficiency of the financial market is not undesirable. It is possible for managers to be paid their *measured* marginal product, Z_t, rather than the expected marginal product. The capital market will then be used as a mechanism for smoothing out the wages over time, so as to approximate the result in (5.12). Note, however, that labor contracts suffer from the same kind of impediments associated with the functioning of the financial markets.

for current marginal products to be approximated by changes in the current value of human capital. It is possible to counter this point by arguing that managerial pension provisions can be designed to accommodate incentive problems of this type, but this itself flies in the face of the spirit of natural, costless market resolution to agency problems. The need for complex provisions in contracts relative to managerial compensation at retirement is at least conceptually similar to the need for complex provisions in financial contracts to compensate for inadequacies in the capital market to resolve agency problems.

Managers can also avoid a complete *ex post* settling up by switching from one firm to another. If all firms have the same information relating to managerial performance, the managers' new firms set their wages according to the same process as the old firms. In this setting, the managers cannot escape the consequences of shriking by switching. However, it seems likely that the new firms know less of the managers' true performance than the old firms, once again providing the opportunity for managers to bury on-the-job consumption.

5.4 Conclusion

In the context of perfectly efficient financial and labor markets, the agency problems associated with bankruptcy, and the incentives to take risk, forgo profitable investments, and consume perquisites are all neutralized. The expected values of the costs associated with these problems are zero and their impact on the valuation of the firm is inconsequential. In this setting, the form and relative magnitudes of financial contracts have no impact on these incentives and the method by which a firm finances its investments is irrelevant.

In general, however, impediments exist to the efficient operation of both the capital and the labor markets. To the extent that these impediments are significant, investors cannot fully rely on markets to resolve the conflicts of interest that exist between the various parties to the firm. They must instead place reliance on complex contracts relating to both managerial compensation and to the nature of the claims of outsiders to the firm's income. Consequently, financial contracting cannot be treated with indifference, and it becomes relevant to the valuation of the firm by the market. In the next chapter, we discuss how financial contracts can be designed so as to resolve the conflicts of interest that exist among securityholders.

Complex Financial Contracts as
Solutions to Agency Problems

6.1 Introduction

As discussed in Chapter 5, financial and labor markets may fail to provide complete and costless solutions to all classes of agency problems analyzed in Chapter 3. In this chapter, we analyze several examples of complex financial contracts that play a role in eliminating any agency problems remaining unresolved by the market place. These complex contracts include call provisions in corporate debt, managerial stock options, convertible debt, income bonds, indenture provisions, pension plans, and corporate bylaws. Thus, many of the popular contractual arrangements that we observe in financial and labor markets can be rationalized on the basis of agency problems.

The following section introduces lessons from the economic theory of agency. In the tradition of the agency theory, the contractual agreement between the principal and the agent specifies an optimal rule for sharing the observed output. The form of this sharing rule varies, depending upon the observability of the policies or efforts taken by the agent. It also varies depending upon the risk attitudes of both the agent and the principal. In the subsequent sections, we are explicit about the nature of financial contracts that specify sharing rules among securityholders with divergent interests. Section 6.3 analyzes a sharing rule implied by call provisions in corporate debt and its rule in resolving agency problems that exist between equityholders as agents and debtholders as principals. Sections 6.4 and 6.5 address sharing rules implied in the issuance of convertible debt and executive stock options, respectively. A simultaneous solution to the excessive per- quisite consumption by an entrepreneur-manager and risk incentive problems through convertible debt and managerial stock options is provided in Section 6.6. The solution is illustrated in an appendix to this chapter. Finally, Section 6.7 takes up other observed complex contracts in financial and labor markets.

6.2 Basic Risk Sharing Rules: Lessons from the Economic Theory of Agency

As an example of the principal–agent relationship, consider clients and lawyers who seek to establish an agency relationship. The terms of the lawyers' compensation pose the core of the issue typically raised in the agency literature. What is the form of the lawyers' compensation schedule? In other words, what variables determine the agent's fee? One thing is clear. The variables must be observable *ex post* by both parties, so that there should be no ambiguity in the amounts payable to lawyers for their legal services.

The immediate variables of interest to lawyers and clients are: a) the efforts expended by the lawyers (e.g., time they spent on the case); b) the outcome of the case; and c) the state of nature or uncertain exogenous events affecting the outcome. The outcome of the case is always presumed observable. Their efforts may not be observable. If both efforts and outcome are observable, the observability of the ef- fects of exogenous factors is redundant. If efforts are not freely ob- servable, then lawyers and clients may seek to employ certain signals or parameters that convey information about the efforts in the prep- aration of the case. Again, these signals must be observable by both parties. For instance, inquiries can be made about the lawyers' efforts in the legal community.

The legal (agency) relationship that exists between lawyers and clients typifies a wide range of agency problems that exist in the real world. Such moral hazard problems exist in insurance markets, financial markets, and labor markets. In the labor markets, the form of man- agerial compensation schedule is an issue to be resolved in the mutual interests of management and shareholders as a group. Now, going back to the lawyer–client relationship, we shall characterize the terms of contractual agreements that must exist under various scenarios.[1]

---

[1] A number of these standard results appear in published papers. See for instance, M. Harris and A. Raviv, "Some Results on Incentive Contracts," *American Economic Review* (March 1978); S. Shavell, "Risk Sharing and Incentives in the Principal and Agent Relationship," *Bell Journal of Economics* (Spring 1979); B. Holmstrom, "Moral Hazard and Observability," *Bell Journal of Economics* (Spring 1979). A direct illustration of these results in designing investment banking contracts appears in D. Baron and B.

6.21 The First-Best Contract

Assume that the efforts expended by lawyers (e) can be expressed as a monetary cost. Lawyers derive disutility from the cost aspect of e. Given a particular state of nature sεS (the efforts of opposing lawyers, the disposition of the judge or jury, etc.) higher levels of effort result in geater output qεQ (the monetary equivalent of the outcome of the case). Clients derive a positive utility from q. They would prefer a greater effort on the lawyers' part, given s. Thus, the parties face a production (output) function q = f(e,s). Their objective is to design a schedule that is optimal in a utility maximizing sense.

Given a specific compensation schedule ϕ(q,k), lawyers maximize their expected utility by exerting a certain level of effort, e. Compensation is scheduled as a function of q and other relevant variables, k, which are observable by both parties. Suppose that the only observable variable is q; then a lawyer's expected utility is a positive function of ϕ and a negative function of e.

Lawyers require a minimum level of expected utility in order to be induced into a legal relationship with clients. This reservation level of utility is determined by a bargaining process or by market forces. In a well-functioning legal environment, lawyers can state the utility level that they can achieve without the contract under similar circumstances. While lawyers must be assured of a minimum level of utility, the compensation contract must induce them to adopt legal strategies that are consistent with the maximization of the client's utility subject to certain additional constraints to be discussed below. If these additional constraints are of no consequence in utility maximization, then we have the "first-best contract" between the parties.

Thus, the first-best contract is a solution to an optimization program that maximizes the client's utility subject to the constraint that the reservation level of the lawyer's expected utility is attained. If the first-best contract exists, it provides the right incentive for lawyers to perform the contract in accordance with maximization of the client's utility. Consequently, an *incentive* problem that leads lawyers to pick the level of effort that maximizes their own utility at the expense of their clients disappears. There are at least two conditions under which the first-best contract is achievable. The first case occurs when the

Holmstrom, "The Investment Banking Contracts for New Issues Under Asymmetric Information: Delegation and the Incentive Problem," *Journal of Finance* (December 1980). Earlier literature in this area includes K. Borch, "Equilibrium in a Reinsurance Market," *Econometrica* Vol 30, No. 3 (1962); S. Ross, "The Economic Theory of Agency: The Principal's Problem," *American Economic Review* (May 1973); J. Mirrlees, "The Optimal Structure of Incentives and Authority Within an Organization," *Bell Journal of Economics* (Spring 1976); R. Zeckhauser, "Medical Insurance: A Case Study of the Trade-Off Between Risk Spreading and Appropriate Incentives," *Journal of Economic Theory*, Vol 2 (March 1970); R. Wilson, "The Theory of Syndicates," *Econometrica*, Vol 36 (January 1968).

lawyers' efforts are freely observable by both parties. Under this condition, the client can dictate a *forcing* contract that is acceptable by the lawyer. For instance, this contract can specify $\phi^*(q,e) = \phi(q)$ if $e = \hat{e}$ and $\phi^*(q,e) = M$ if $e \neq \hat{e}$. In other words, a forcing contract provides a fee schedule conditioned on the prespecified level of the efforts to be taken by lawyers. If the observed efforts are at variance with the contractual efforts, lawyers are penalized to the extent of $M < 0$. The penalty can be made large enough, so as to force the lawyer to expend the efforts preferred by the clients, and at the same time $\phi(q)$ can be picked to provide an optimal sharing rule. If the lawyers' efforts are freely observable, a forcing contract can exist to achieve the first-best solution irrespective of the risk attitudes of the parties involved.[2]

The second case under which the first-best contract exists is when the lawyers are risk neutral. Their efforts need not be observed if they are risk neutral. The contract takes a form whereby clients are rewarded a fixed payoff, and lawyers obtain the remaining share, which varies with the outcome of the case. Thus, the lawyers are rewarded $\phi^*(q,e) = q - F$, where F is the fixed payment to the client.[3] On the other hand, fixed payoffs alone to lawyers are improper, because they would find it optimal to expend no efforts in the case. Note that their efforts are not observable under this scenario. However, risk neutral lawyers have a proper incentive to employ their best efforts if they are rewarded a fee dependent on the outcome minus a fixed commitment to their clients. Nonetheless, there is no gain from observing their efforts, because they are willing to absorb the entire risk anyway. The observability of their effort is useful in reducing the variability of their compensation, given the effort. But this variability is of no concern to them due to their risk neutral attitude.[4]

6.22 The Second-Best Contract

The preceding contract is no longer optimal if lawyers are risk averse and their efforts are not freely observable. With free observability, of course, clients can dictate forcing contracts that are acceptable to lawyers. Their risk aversion alone does not preclude the first-best fee schedule. On the other hand, if their efforts are observed with ambiguity, risk averse lawyers will choose to share part of the uncertainty with clients. Therefore, an incentive exists for them to take actions that are not in the best interests of their clients, given an

---

[2] Our discussion here has focused on the *form* of the contract. It is fairly tricky to obtain an exact solution. See J. Mirrlees, *ibid.*; B. Holmstrom, *ibid.*

[3] The proof that the contract achieves the first-best sharing rule is provided in Shavell, "Risk Sharing," Appendix, p. 90.

[4] Both first-best solutions assume away any probability of default on the part of the agent with respect to either payment of the penalty, M, or with respect to the fixed payment, F.

arbitrary fee schedule ϕ. Thus, a solution to the program, which satisfies only the constraint that the lawyers receive the reservation utility can no longer neutralize the lawyer's incentive problem. The optimization program must be expanded to include another restriction which recognizes that the lawyers will pick the effort level that maximizes their own expected utility.

The contract that evolves from the solution to the expanded program can be shown to be Pareto-inferior to the contract specified in the earlier section. Hence, it is the "second-best contract."[5] Throughout our discussion, two important assumptions are implicit. First, lawyers and clients know each others' utility function. Second, they do not engage in a mutually *destructive* bargaining process in designing the contract. The optimal solution exists when it is no longer possible to improve either party's welfare without impairing the welfare of the other. Others have demonstrated that costless and informative signals about the effort of lawyers have the property of improving the contract.[6] Indeed, if perfect signals exist, a forcing contract can again be used. If imperfect signals exist, the fee schedule must depend not only on the outcome but also on the informational content of the signal.

The following sections turn to the main thrust of the chapter. We examine financial contractual relationships that exist among the firm's securityholders with divergent interests. An agency theoretic rationale is provided for various complex financial contracts that are observed in the real world. These contracts play a vital role in providing optimal sharing rules among the securityholders in a principal-agent relationship. The framework utilized in the following sections recognizes the existence of financial markets, unlike the prevailing economic theory of agency. The existence of financial markets provides an opportunity to neutralize or mitigate the risk sharing problem characterizing the single agent–principal relationship discussed earlier.

---

[5] The expanded optimization program can be stated as:

$$\text{Max}_{\phi} \ E_s \ V(\phi,e) = \int V[\phi(q,e)]f(s)ds \tag{A}$$

s.t.

$$E_s \ U(\phi,e) \geq U_o \tag{B}$$

$$\text{Max}_c \ E_s \ U(\phi,e) = \int U[\phi(q),e]f(s)ds \tag{C}$$

where

V and U are utilities characterizing clients and lawyers, respectively.

The solution to the expanded program may not exist. See Mirrlees, *ibid*. It is usually assumed that the first-order condition $[E_s U_c(\phi,e) = 0]$ identifies the solution to the above program.

[6] See, for instance, Holmstrom "Moral Hazard" and Shavell "Risk Sharing."

For instance, entrepreneurs as agents can raise funds from external capital contributors (or principals) without worrying about the risk sharing problem, because they can diversify risk directly through the financial markets. Moreover, in many instances, our framework recognizes limited liability provisions characterizing real-life financial contracts, unlike the first-best contract in the standard economic theory of agency, which is predicated on unlimited liability. Also, under some conditions, these financial contracts may not be first-best, but an agency theory, nonetheless, provides a powerful explanation for their existence. This is important in light of the unfortunate fact that popular textbook explanations for complex contracts are based on implicit market irrationality or an impeded arbitrage process in the market.

6.3 Callable Debt

There is no such thing as a free call. Despite this glaring fact, traditional finance rationalizes call provisions in corporate debt as a mechanism for stockholders to reap the increase in bond value during periods of declining interest rates. This theft is consummated by simply retiring the debt at a predetermined call price. Thus, bondholders lose commensurately because they are assumed to be ignorant. On the other hand, it is not clever to assume that stockholders are systematically smarter than bondholders, or vice-versa. It is safer to assume that intelligence is independent of the form of securities held. Under this safe assumption, bondholders recognize that a callable debt is a complex security consisting of a positive position in a noncallable debt and a negative position in call option retained by stockholders. Obviously, bondholders do not offer this call option free of charge. When arbitrage profits are fully exploited, the value of a callable bond must be equal to the value of the underlying noncallable bond minus the value of the call privilege. Thus, at issuance, stockholders are charged an amount that reflects the full value of the call privilege.

Why then issue a callable debt when the call is no longer a free good? Unfortunately we cannot find any rationale in the traditional framework.[7] However, we saw in Chapter 3 that straight (noncallable) debt financing precipitates agency problems whose consequences are entirely borne by stockholders (agents). In other words, a noncallable debt can be harmful to equityholders without harming debtholders.

---

[7] The conventional framework includes the original Modigliani-Miller theorem as well as extensions into the tax world. For instance, see F. Modigliani and M. Miller, "The Cost of Capital, Corporation Finance, and the Theory of Investment," *American Economic Review* (June 1958); J. Stiglitz, "On the Irrelevance of Corporate Financial Policy," *American Economic Review* (December 1974); M. Miller, "Debt and Taxes," *Journal of Finance* (May 1977).

It is harmful because debtholders discount all the relevant agency costs in pricing noncallable debt. In this section we wish to demonstrate how call provisions in corporate debt can mitigate, or even eliminate, the costs engendered by issuing "naked" debt. Thus, call provisions can improve stockholder position without impairing bondholder welfare.

6.31 Callable Debt and Informational Asymmetry

Suppose that the firm is worth $V(A)$. However, the market is unable to distinguish it from another lesser firm B with value $V(B)$ where $V(A) > V(B)$. If management seeks to raise debt capital, the value of a noncallable debt is $V_D(A)$ with the presumption that the firm is worth $V(A)$, but it drops to $V_D(B)$ if the firm is presumed to be valued at $V(B)$. Suppose that the debt is due to mature in T periods and the true nature of the firm is to be revealed to the market at some point prior to the debt maturity.[8] The agency cost of informational asymmetry is $V_D(A) - V_D(B)$.[9] The firm can reduce this cost through the use of a call option.

The call privilege entitles the issuer of the bond to a premature retirement. For the sake of simplicity, consider a scenario in which the true nature of a firm (A or B) is revealed at $t = 1$, and that the call option is also exercisable at $t = 1$. At that time, the value, $V_D(s)$, of the underlying *noncallable* debt depends on the prevailing state of nature s. Also, for purposes of exposition only, assume that the debt matures at $t = 2$, at which time the value of its noncallable analog, $V(z)$, depends upon the *second period* states of nature, z, revealed at $t = 2$. Thus, at $t = 1$

$$V_D(s) = \int_z p(z|s) \min [V(z|s), F] d(z|s) \qquad (6.1)$$

---

[8] It is assumed here that management serves in the best interests of *all* stockholders, including new equity capital contributors. In a more general framework, asymmetry of information arises whenever new capital is to be raised. We assume away the problem with new equity capital so as to focus on the agency problem of debt financing.

[9] Under certain conditions informational asymmetry may be resolved, at a cost, through various signaling mechanisms as discussed in the literature. S. Ross, "The Determination of Financial Structure: The Incentive-Signaling Approach," *The Bell Journal of Economics* (Spring 1977), argues that, if a managerial incentive schedule is properly specified, the financial structure of the firm can serve as a signal. H. Leland and D. Pyle, in "Informational Asymmetries, Financial Structure, and Financial Intermediation," *Journal of Finance* (May 1977), on the other hand, employ the entrepreneur's equity stake as a signal. The limitations of these signaling mechanisms are discussed in R. Haugen and L. Senbet, "New Perspectives on Informational Asymmetry and Agency Relationships," *Journal of Financial and Quantitative Analysis* (November 1979), who also seek to provide *joint* solutions to informational asymmetry and agency problems. Unlike Ross, Leland, and Pyle, Haugen and Senbet also argue that signaling through the financial structure of the firm is costly. Like Ross, though, Haugen and Senbet assume that the entrepreneur is not allowed to trade in the liabilities of the firm. This is in accordance with certain observable legalities that prevent managers from trading in their own firm's liabilities so as to avoid moral hazard problems.

where

$p(z|s)$ = the z-state price given that s, the state of nature at $t = 1$, is revealed.

$V(z|s)$ = the z-state contingent value of the firm, given that s has occurred at $t = 1$.

F = the face value of the debt, which is assumed to be a pure discount bond.

The debt will be called (or the call option will be exercised) at $t = 1$ whenever $V_D(s) > P$. The corresponding current value of the call privilege can be expressed at $t = 0$ as

$$V_C = \int_s p(s) \max[0, V_D(s) - P]ds \qquad (6.2)$$

In the preceding framework, the corresponding value of a callable bond must be equal to the value of the underlying noncallable bond less the value of the call privilege. Therefore, it can be written at $t = 0$ as

$$V_D^* = \int_s p(s) V_D(s)ds - V_C \qquad (6.3)$$

It is interesting to note that the maximum value of V_D^* in (6.3) collapses to the discounted value of P, given (6.1) and (6.2). The maximum that bondholders pay for a callable debt is the discounted value of the call price, because this special case obtains when $V_D(s) > P$ for all states of nature, or when the bond is sure to be called. Indeed, the callable bond price $V_D^*(s)$ must equal P at $t = 1$ whenever $V_D(s) > P$. One should also note that P can be less than F in our framework, contrary to the existing practice. While we deal with a pure discount bond here, the existing call provisions are attached to more complex coupon bonds, each of which can be regarded as a pure discount bond. In what follows, we demonstrate how the problem of informational asymmetry can be mitigated by employing P as a decision variable. We wish to emphasize again that the optimal value of this variable is critically dependent on the nature of the underlying bond offered, as well as the underlying project to be financed.

In the absence of informational asymmetry and agency problems, there is no possibility of wealth transfer among the securityholders, and hence the issuer is indifferent between the callable and the non-callable issue. However, such is not the case when you, as an entrepreneur, suffer from the consequences of informational asymmetry. The value of a call privilege associated with A, $V_C(A)$, exceeds that of B, $V_C(B)$. While you suffer in the form of the discrepancy between $V_D(A)$ and $V_D(B)$, you can recapture part of it through the issuance of a callable debt in the amount of $(V_C(A) - V_C(B))$. Thus, there

revelation
period of
true value
is imp.

exists a definite preference for the issuance of callable debt in an environment characterized by information asymmetry.[10]

It should be pointed out that the call feature mitigates a transfer of wealth only to the extent that the true nature of the firm is revealed prior to the maturity of the debt. To maximize the benefit associated with the call, the expiration date for the call provision must immediately follow revelation of the true nature of the firm. The sooner that this revelation occurs, the more effective the call option in preventing expropriation of stockholder wealth by bondholders. If the revelation period is extremely small and the expiration period is of a corresponding length, nearly all of the wealth transfer can be avoided. If, however, the revelation period is equal to the term to maturity on the bonds, none of the wealth transfer is avoided. If the call date and maturity dates are equal, adding a call feature (with an exercise price less than the face value) is equivalent to merely reducing the amount (rather than the maturity) of debt in the capital structure, which obviously is a nonsolution to the asymmetry problem. Thus, the call has an optimal expiration period that relates to the timing of the release of information associated with the asset being financed.[11]

6.32 The Risk Incentive Costs of Debt

Call provisions in corporate debt can also be used to eliminate agency problems associated with shifting the risk of underlying assets. Risk shifting problems were discussed in Chapter 3. We now wish to demonstrate the role of call provisions in resolving these incentive problems.

Suppose that management of a growth firm seeks to finance a capital expenditure program (call it A), but an alternative investment opportunity B is available, which is riskier [i.e., $\sigma(B) > \sigma(A)$]. However, B is less valuable, so that $\Delta V = V(B) - V(A) < 0$. We assume that the two investment opportunities require equal initial cost outlay. Under this scenario, there may exist an incentive for management to

---

[10] The wealth recaptured through the increased value of a call privilege occurs without impairing the amount of financing needed. Given F and project B, an identical amount of debt capital can be raised with both a callable and a noncallable contract if the call privilege is made worthless by adjusting P. As shown in equation (6.2), $V_C = 0$, if $P > V_D(s)$ for all s. Note that $V_D(s)$ itself is constrained by (6.1), and it is a finite amount so long as F is finite. Depending upon P, this call privilege is worthy in the context of project A but worthless in the context of project B. Thus, you as an entrepreneur are able to recapture part of the cost of informational asymmetry through the increased value of a call privilege. Given the amount of financing needed and the associated F, determining P is a constrained optimization problem in which $V_C(A)$ is maximized subject to the constraint that $V_C(B) = 0$.

[11] The solution via a call provision cannot signal out the true current value of the firm, but it can serve as a means of recapturing (at least partially) the welfare loss to the entrepreneur induced by informational asymmetry. The residual loss not recaptured by a call provision is, of course, analogous to the cost associated with a signaling mechanism.

riskier

shift to B if debtholders provide $V_D(A)$ with the presumption that A would be adopted, because the incremental value of equity associated with the shift may be positive. In the parlance of Figure 6.1A, the stockholders will shift to the risky project when $\Delta V_s = V_s(B) - V_s(A) > 0$. In other words, the net effect of the shift on equity value is

Figure 6.1. Resolving the Risk Incentive Problem with Callable Debt

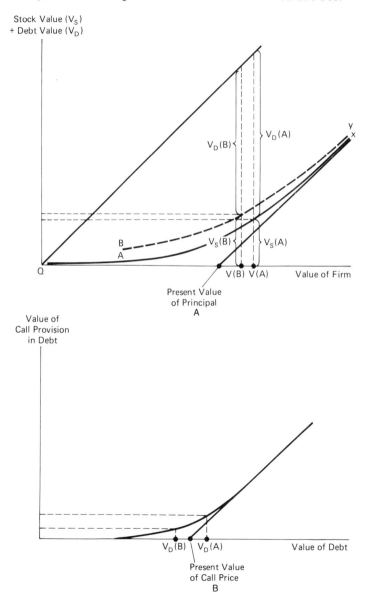

positive. This net effect is the difference between the incremental effect of increased variance and the *decremental* effect of the reduced value of the underlying assets.

Consider Figure 6.1A. The value of the firm is depicted on the horizontal axis while the debt and equity (V_s) values are shown on the vertical axis. The curve OX is drawn with the presumption that the equity of the firm is valued in accordance with the Black-Scholes model and investment opportunity A is chosen. The curve OY is drawn under the presumption that the higher variance project B is chosen.[12] Since debt is a complement of equity, vertical differences between the 45-degree line OZ and OX depict debt values. With rational expectations, debtholders again recognize the incentive problem and discount the debt value accordingly, such that they would offer $V_D(B)$ and not $V_D(A)$ in return for their claim. In the absence of mechanisms that resolve the incentive problem, management incurs the agency costs in the amount of $V(A) - V(B)$.

It is in the best interests of management to seek contracts that eliminate the incentive to shift to high-risk, low-value projects. Figure 6.1B depicts the value of a call option written on the bonds of the firm. The issuance of debt with such a call provision accomplishes the purpose of eliminating the risk incentive. The value of a call privilege associated with A is higher than the one associated with B for the same call price. The rationale for this is provided earlier, in connection with Figure 6.1A, where the call privilege pricing function is presumed to be specified in accordance with the Black-Scholes option pricing model. The solution to the incentive problem is to design the call price (i.e., the exercise price) such that the change in equity value is offset by the change in the value of the call privilege, as it is in Figure 6.1. In the parlance of Figure 6.1, this occurs when $\Delta V_C = \Delta V_s$ in absolute terms. It may be more instructive to characterize the role of a call provision contract in neutralizing the risk shifting incentive effect by the following numerical example. This example is designed to correspond closely with Figure 6.1 for a given investment opportunity set and promised debt obligation. As in Figure 6.1, the incentive effect

---

[12] J. Long, in "Discussion," *Journal of Finance* (May 1977), points out the difficulty in applying the model for the pricing of corporate liabilities, if the total value of the firm is dependent on its capital structure. This dependence occurs because the probability distribution of the future cash flows may be affected by bankruptcy costs and tax subsidies, and hence, the stochastic process underlying the total value of the firm cannot be specified without reference to the prices of the firm's bonds. The functional dependence leads to a nonlinear differential equation, leading to the difficulty in obtaining the bond pricing formula. In light of Long's argument, we follow the tradition (e.g., Jensen and Meckling, "Theory of the Firm") and use the Black-Scholes model *qualitatively* wherever applicable in this chapter.

of risk shifting ($90) is exactly offset by the corresponding incentive effect on the value of the call privilege ($-$90). For convenience we have allowed the amount of debt financing with a callable contract to decline, but it is possible to design a contract where the financing required through the debt marker is fixed. Note also that the agency cost under a *noncallable* contract is $100, which would be borne entirely by the agents (existing equityholders).

	Under a Noncallable Contract		Under a Callable Contract	
Risk:	$\sigma(A) = .05$	$\sigma(B) = 0.10$	$\sigma(A) = 0.05$	$\sigma(B) = 0.10$
Values:	$V(A) = \$1000$	$V(B) = \$900$	$V(A) = \$1000$	$V(B) = \$900$
	$V_D(A) = 800$	$V_D(B) = 610$	$V_D(A) = 800$	$V_D(B) = 610$
	$V_S(A) = 200$	$V_S(B) = 290$	$V_C(A) = 100$	$V_C(B) = 10$
Incentive Effect of Risk Shifting:	$V_S(B) - V_S(A) = \Delta V_S = \$90$		$V_D^*(A) = 700 \quad V_D^*(B) = 600$	
			$V_S^*(A) = 300 \quad V_S^*(B) = 300$	
			Incentive effect on the value of the call privilege:	
Agency cost:	$V(A) - V(B) = \$100$		$V_C(B) - V_C(A) = -\$90$	
			Therefore:	
			$V_S^*(B) - V_S^*(A) = 0$	
Definition:		$V_D^* = V_D - V_C =$	Value of a callable debt	
		$V_S^* = V - V_D^* =$	Value of the stock associated with a callable contract	

Thus, the issuance of a callable debt with an appropriate call price resolves the agency problem associated with risk shifting. Since the risk incentive problem is neutralized, management can raise debt in the amount of $V_D^*(A)$. Consequently, the process of eliminating this important class of agency problems provides a strong economic rationale for the existence of call provisions in corporate debt.

6.33 Callable Debt and The Incentive to Reject Profitable Future Investment Opportunities

We now argue that agency problems associated with the incentive to forgo otherwise profitable future investment opportunities can also be resolved through call provisions in corporate debt. Recall that these problems are discussed in Chapter 3. One aspect of these problems arises when the firm already carries debt associated with financing of existing assets (or assets in place). When growth opportunities surface in the future, they may lead to uncompensated shifts in wealth to existing bondholders. This particular problem is addressed in the literature, and it can be demonstrated that a call provision in the debt increases the welfare of shareholders.[13]

The other aspect of growth opportunity problems arises when currently issued debt is entirely supported by a growth opportunity. This is the agency problem associated with Figure 3.4 in Chapter 3. This problem, unlike the preceding problem, cannot be eliminated through the issuance of debt with a conventional call provision. This is because the debt itself is entirely supported, and issued against, the growth opportunity. This is a phenomenon not readily observed in the real world, and hence it begs a solution that is not readily observable. One feasible solution is to issue callable debt with a stochastic call price conditioned on the profitability of the investment opportunity.[14] Suppose that the debt contract is written with the provision that the debt be called when $V(s) - I < P$ at a call price that is equal to $\max[0, \alpha(V(s) - I)]$, where $0 < \alpha < 1$. Or, alternatively, the debt is callable at $\alpha(V(s) - I)$ when $V(S) - I < P$ but $V(s) > I$. This call strategy can fully restore the value of the firm.[15] The call provision aligns the interests of both bondholders and stockholders in terms of following the optimal investment strategy. Consequently, the value of the firm can be restored as

$$V = V_D'' + V_M' = \int_{s_a}^{\infty} q(s) [V(s) - I] ds \qquad (6.4)$$

where

$$V_D'' = V_D' + \int_{s_a}^{s_b} q(s) (1 - \alpha) [V(s) - I] ds = \text{the value of debt}$$

$$V_M' = V_M + \int_{s_a}^{s_b} q(s) \alpha [V(s) - I] ds \qquad = \text{the value of equity}$$

[13] See Z. Bodie and R. Taggart, "Future Investment Opportunities and the Value of the Call Provision on a Bond," *Journal of Finance* (September 1978) for further discussion on this point. With the exception of a special numerical example, their general result with callable debt may not restore the value of the firm to that which exists under all-equity financing in which investments have positive net present value. Nonetheless, the issuance of callable debt is shown to stochastically dominate the case of a noncallable debt, and hence a strong case is established for the inclusion of a call provision in all corporate debt contracts.

[14] It is tempting to argue that bondholders and stockholders can renegotiate the debt contract, so as to avoid the growth opportunity problem. Such an argument is contained in V. Aivazian and J. Callen, "Corporate Leverage and Growth: The Game Theoretic Issues," *Journal of Financial Economics* (December 1980). This argument is valid if renegotiation is costless. However, this merely sterilizes the problem, because all agency problems must disappear in a market structure that permits free and costless renegotiation of contracts!

[15] The issue in S. Myers, "Determinants of Corporate Borrowing," *Journal of Financial Economics* (November 1977) can also be resolved through the use of convertible or "puttable" bonds. Puttable bonds are issued by the U.S. Government (e.g., E and H Savings Bonds), but they are not commonly observed in the private sector. Nonetheless,

and V_D' and V_M are original debt and equity values, respectively, with unresolved agency problems.

As a closing remark, we wish to point out that structuring the debt maturity accomplishes the same task as the call strategy. This is not surprising, because the call provision can be viewed as a mechanism of shortening the expected value of the life of the debt contract. In this context, the essential difference between short-term debt and a callable long-term debt arises with respect to uncertainty about the date of premature retirement.[16] Therefore, the process of eliminating these important classes of agency problems also provides a rationale for the existence of multiple maturities and call provisions in corporate debt. It is often suggested in the literature, however, that differential transaction costs alone rationalize the existence of preferred maturity at an individual firm level. We find this view to be inconsistent with equilibrium in the bond market, because it ignores the possibility that, in equilibrium, bonds of different maturity are priced to yield differential returns so as to reflect transaction costs.

6.4 Convertible Debt

There is no such a thing as a free put. In a single period context, a convertible bond is a composite of a stock and a put option granting the bondholder the right to sell the stock back to the firm at an exercise price equal to the prevailing value of the bond. Exercise of the put is tantamount to not converting and retaining the bond to receive its associated fixed payments. Failure to exercise is tantamount to converting and ending up with the stock alone.

According to a popular textbook explanation, convertible bond financing is intended to serve as a mechanism for deferred equity financing. This deferral is presumed to reduce potential dilution in earnings per share that would have been associated with current equity financing at a "depressed" market price. When conversion presumably occurs in the future at the time of more favorable stock prices, the dilution is mitigated. This requires a conversion price that is substantially higher than the current "depressed" value of shares of stock to be exchanged for a bond. In terms of our put-stock analog to the convertible bond, this implies that the number of shares associated with the put-stock package will be relatively small. Suppose, however, that the current market price of the stock is an outcome of rational

---

companies, such as the Beneficial Corporation and Blyth Eastman are known to issue such bonds. See W. Boyce and A. Kalotay, "Tax Differentials and Callable Bonds," *Journal of Finance* (September 1979) for further information on puttable bonds.

[16] The details about the role of debt maturity structure in resolving specific agency problems are provided in A. Barnea, R. Haugen, and L. Senbet, "A Rationale for Debt Maturity Structure and Call Provisions in the Agency Theoretic Framework," *Journal of Finance* (December 1980).

price determination reflecting future expectations. It is then very likely that the put will be exercised in the future. That is, convertible bondholders sell the stock that they *already* own (as implicit in the convertible debt) at an exercise (conversion) price, which is presumably set high enough, in an attempt to raise delayed equity financing with a minimum of dilution (recall that the number of shares on the package is small). Conversion need not occur, nor does deferred equity financing.

Another popular textbook explanation rationalizes convertible bond financing as a means of raising debt at lower interest rates than straight debt. This is also an irrational explanation. A convertible bond can be alternatively viewed as a composite of straight bond and a call option to buy the underlying stock at a conversion price. Note that, unlike the traditional exercise price on an option, the conversion price is state-dependent, for it is the value of a bond (if it were straight) given up to obtain the predetermined number of shares of stock. In this sense, we use the prevailing bond value and the conversion price interchangeably. At any rate, the lower interest rate on a convertible bond is a mere compensation to current equityholders for writing the option embodied in a convertible bond. Recall that a call option is not a free good. While in the previous scenario the value of the implicit put option is a positive function of the conversion price, the value of the implicit call option is a negative function of the conversion price. The put has value in the event of unprofitable conversion, but the call is worthless in this case. Note also that the value of convertible debt converges to the value of straight debt as the conversion price increases. If bondholders are rational and are willing to pay an appropriate amount for their conversion privilege, and if there are no agency problems, the firm should be indifferent toward issuing convertible versus nonconvertible debt.

What, then, is a rationale for convertible debt? We wish to demonstrate that convertible debt, like callable debt, can play a vital role in resolving agency problems associated with external capital. When we examined the role of callable debt in the preceding section, we excluded the agency problem of consuming perquisites (perks). The nature of the perk problem was discussed in Chapter 3, but here we shall see that the problem can be resolved through convertible debt. Suppose you, as owner-manager, offer a put option to be retained by external capital contributors to sell the entire firm at a stated price, E_p, at the termination of the productive period. Thus, the financing package includes a sale of $(1 - \alpha)$ fraction of equity and a put option. The put option has the potential to eliminate your incentive to consume perks, because your perk consumption increases your liability to external equityholders.

Equityholders hold positive positions in the stock and the put. This combined position is equivalent to selling or taking a negative position in a convertible bond, although here its feature is somewhat different from the conventional convertible security whose conversion (exercise) price is not deterministic. Recall that in our framework, the conversion feature arises in the following sense. If the terminal value of the firm exceeds the stated price on the put option, the option is worthless, but outsiders remain as common stockholders with partial interests in the firm. This is analogous to conversion into common stock. If the value of the firm falls below the exercise price, the put is exercised and outsiders sell the entire firm to you at the exercise price. This event is analogous to convertible bondholders failing to convert and exercising their fixed claim.

Turning now to the role of convertible debt in resolving the perk problems, we modify Figure 3.2 in Chapter 3, so as to consider the effect of the complex financial package on your wealth opportunity trade-off as owner-manager. Consider Figure 6.2, whose left-hand side is similar to that of the original Jensen-Meckling analysis. Line $\overline{VF}$ depicts the total value of the firm as a function of perquisite consumption F. This line represents the relationship between dollar wealth and perk consumption for you as a manager and *sole* owner. As sole owner, you maximize utility at the tangency point (V*, F*) between the wealth line and your indifference curve. Of course, as we demonstrated in Chapter 3, as partial owner you suffer a utility loss so as to bear the agency cost associated with raising external equity capital.

Fortunately, you can improve your welfare as partial owner without impairing the interests of external financiers by altering the financing package. If the financing package includes convertible debt, your wealth opportunity locus moves up to V'Q'. This augmented wealth line is generated by superimposing the put option value, (V_p), which is depicted on the right hand side of Figure 6.2, as a function of firm value (V). Assume that the put option is valued after taking account of the possibility of default on payment of the exercise price. The augmented wealth line can be expressed as

$$V_W = V_S + \alpha V - V_p \qquad (6.5)$$

where

V_S = outside capital needed and contributed (this is assumed fixed throughout the chapter).

The zero agency cost solution requires that the point (V*, F*) lie on the augmented wealth line, and hence the following conditions must be satisfied. First, your total wealth as owner-manager, including receipts from external capital contributors, must sum up to V*. We call this the *budget constraint.*

$$V_W = V_S + \alpha V^* - V_P = V^* \qquad (6.6)$$

Figure 6.2. Resolving the Perk Incentive Problem with a Put Option

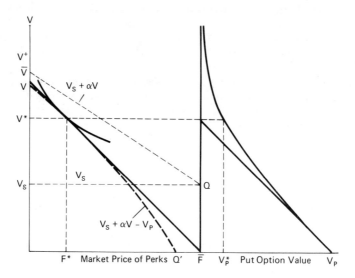

Second, the slope of the wealth line with respect to firm value (V) must equal 1 at V*. We call this the *perk constraint*

$$\left.\frac{\partial V_W}{\partial V}\right|_{V^*} = 1 = \alpha - \left.\frac{\partial V_P}{\partial V}\right|_{V^*} \tag{6.7}$$

or

$$\left.\frac{\partial V_P}{\partial V}\right|_{V^*} = \alpha - 1$$

where the partial derivatives are evaluated at $V^* = \overline{V} - F^* =$ the total firm value at the zero agency cost solution.

The perk constraint is intended to ensure that you as owner-manager consume no excess perquisites beyond what is optimal if you were the sole owner. In other words, the cost to you of consuming a dollar of perks is entirely borne by you in the form of a commensurate change in your wealth (V_W) at a utility maximizing point (V^*, F^*)[17] in Figure 6.2. If you reduce the value of the firm by increasing the consumption of perquisites, you not only reduce the value of your fractional interest in the firm, but you also increase the value of the put option, which is liability to you. The combined effect is to reduce the value of your wealth dollar for dollar with the reduction in the value of the firm.

---

[17] The second-order condition depends on your utility function, but we assume that the condition is satisfied.

We have two equations, (6.6) and (6.7), and two unknowns, α, your fractional ownership interest, and E_p, the exercise price for the put retained by outsiders. Unfortunately, the world is not that simple. Two problems surface immediately. First, we are not assured that the market will price the option so as to simultaneously meet the two equations (constraints), (6.6) and (6.7). Second, the put option creates a "perverse" risk incentive problem. That is, as owner-manager, you now have an incentive to seek *low* variance investment programs in setting up the firm. By so doing, you reduce the value of the put and the corresponding liability to you. Of course, with rational expectations, outsiders recognize this incentive problem and you bear the consequences. In essence, by attempting to solve the perk problem you end up creating another agency problem!

The first problem can be addressed by positing an explicit pricing function for the put. For instance, one can employ the Black-Scholes option pricing model in solving for the two unknowns, α and E_p. Given the validity of the model, the underlying asset return distribution, and the financing requirement, (V_S), explicit solutions may be derived.[18]

In our opinion, the second problem is more serious, but it is a blessing in disguise. The problem is addressed in Section 6.6, where matters become more complex. At the outset, let us recognize that the put option creates an incentive for you to adopt low-risk projects but if managers themselves hold call options this creates a *countervailing* risk incentive. When we mix the two together, we create a financing package that has the potential not only to resolve the perk problem but the risk incentive problem as well. Indeed, our objective in the final section of this chapter is to demonstrate that such a mix provides a rationale for the existence of a complex capital structure in which certain complex financial contracts *coexist* so as to mitigate several classes of agency problems simultaneously. Now you can see why these problems constitute a blessing in disguise, because, frankly, their resolution clears up certain puzzles that have existed in finance for quite some time. We shall discuss this further in Section 6.6.

6.5 Executive Stock Options

As an owner-executive, you can also employ *call* options to align your interests with those of outside securityholders insofar as perk consumption is concerned. You offer a financial package in which you hold a fractional interest in equity but retain a call option to buy back the entire firm at E_C. This use of the call option is analogous to

---

[18] R. Haugen and L. Senbet, in "Resolving the Agency Problems of External Capital through Stock Options," *Journal of Finance* (June 1981), show that explicit solutions may be derived under more general conditions. R. Green, in "Investment Incentives, Debt, and Warrants," *Journal of Financial Economics* (March 1984) , extends the use of convertible bonds into the case of limited liability provisions.

Figure 6.3. The Use of a Call Option to Resolve the Perk Problem

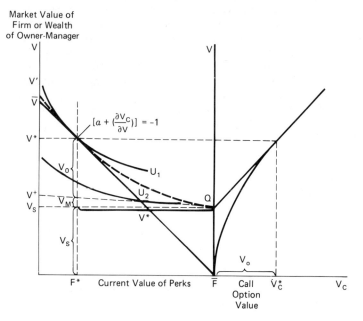

the use of executive stock options in managerial compensation in actual practice.

In our framework, the call option is not marketable, and it must be retained.[19] Again, this is analogous to observed stock option plans. In a typical qualified stock option, the executive is granted an option to exercise at a stated price, which is usually equivalent to the market value of the stock at the date of the grant. The shares under the option are usually nonexercisable before specific dates, which are distributed over a five-year period. The option is also typically non-marketable. A slightly different form of compensation commonly found in practice is the stock appreciation right. This gives the right for an executive to receive compensation based on the difference between the market value of the stock and a preestablished price at a specific expiration date. The compensation may be in the form of cash, stock, or some combination of the two. Stock appreciation rights are sometimes issued in conjunction with nonqualified stock options, in which

---

[19] It should be noted that if you, as manager, are to hold options as well as common shares in the firm, some guarantee must be provided that you will *retain* these securities, at least until the relevant decisions are made and, hence, maintain an alliance with the interests of outside capital contributors. This same problem exists within the Jensen-Meckling framework under common stock financing alone. That is, some guarantee must be made to outside stockholders that you as owner-manager will not dilute your interests in the firm or neutralize your position with a portfolio adjustment.

case, the exercise of either the right or the option cancels the other. Some stock appreciation rights limit the amount of appreciation for which the executive is eligible. Such a limitation is usually not present in a stock option plan. Stock appreciation rights avoid the necessity of an outlay by the executive and also avoid the holding period rule that applies to stock *ownership* under the rules of the Securities and Exchange Commission as defined in the Internal Revenue Code 422(b).

6.51 The Impact of the Call Option

Again we modify Figure 3.2 in Chapter 3 to generate the augmented wealth line V'Q in Figure 6.3. The modified wealth line, V'Q, is drawn by adding the call option value, (V_C), which appears on the right-hand side of Figure 6.3 as a function of V, to the fixed value of V_S and the value of the entrepreneurs' stock, αV. The zero agency cost solution point (V*, F*) must satisfy the following budget and perk constraints, respectively.[20]

$$\text{a)} \quad V_W = V_S + \alpha V* + V_C = V* \tag{6.8}$$

and

$$\text{b)} \quad \left.\frac{\partial V_W}{\partial V}\right|_{V*} = \alpha + \left.\frac{\partial V_C}{\partial V}\right|_{V*} = 1 \tag{6.9}$$

Using this strategy, we run into the same sort of problems associated with the put option when we employ the call option *alone* as a mech-

---

[20] It is conceivable that the augmented wealth line V_5Q may cross the indifference curve U_1 between the tangency point and the intersection at V_5. This depends on the relative convexity of V_5Q and U_1. If the problem exists, it can be overcome either by a put option or by combined use of a call and a put option, as explained in the next section. A sufficient (but not necessary) condition for the value of an option to be a convex function of the stock price is that the distribution of the returns on the stock is independent of the price level. Our analysis does not invoke any particular option pricing model other than the convexity requirement. For instance, if the Black-Scholes model is deemed appropriate to value the options employed in this chapter, the analysis is still intact. However, there are complications with the Black-Scholes model if the firm value is dependent on its capital structure. If so, a more general option pricing function is appropriate for which our analysis still holds.

It should be apparent that if the contract is *continuously* readjusted, outside capital contributors end up holding a riskless position in the firm. However, the solution does not call for continuous readjustments. The contract may be viewed as a solution to the single period world of Jensen and Meckling, in which decisions relating to investment, financing, and the nature of the productive process are made simultaneously at the beginning of the period and are not altered throughout the productive period. Moreover, the contract is readily generalizable to a multiperiod framework where *discrete* time readjustments of contractual positions are feasible, given that the productive decisions and the corresponding incentive problems occur through discrete time.

anism to resolve the perk problem.[21] Since the financial package is conceptually equivalent to the issuance of *risky debt* by you as owner-executive, where you hold all the common stock of the firm and a fraction α of the debt securities, it creates the well-known risk incentive problem associated with debt financing.

6.6 The Simultaneous Resolution of the Perk and the Risk Incentive Problems

The preceding two sections underscore the fact that convertible debt and executive stock options can be rationalized as mechanisms to resolve the problem of managerial perquisite consumption. However, these financial contracts achieve the goal of mitigating the perk problem by creating risk incentive problems, if they are employed arbitrarily. Executive stock options create an incentive for you as an executive to seek high-risk investment assets in setting up the firm. On the other hand, the put option representing convertible debt creates an incentive for you to seek low-risk investment programs. Neither convertible debt securities *alone* nor executive stock options *alone* do the job of eliminating the two classes of agency problems simultaneously. You must offer a complex financial package with a combined put and call option strategy. It is our purpose here to demonstrate that convertible debt and executive stock options, by serving as countervailing forces, can resolve the perk and risk incentive problems simultaneously. This requires the *coexistence* of the two classes of securities in a capital structure, and hence it provides an economic rationale for observed complex financial structure.

We shall illustrate a simultaneous solution to the risk and perk incentive problems by using a particular pricing function for the put and call options. We shall assume first that the capital market is dominated by investors who are risk neutral. Moreover, we shall assume a single period analysis where the terminal value of the firm is uniformly distributed over values $[V_1, V_2]$, where $V_2 > V_1$.[22]

The solution must satisfy three conditions: a) the manager consumes no excess perquisites beyond what is optimal for the sole owner [the perk constraint]; (b) the total wealth of the manager, including

---

[21] The call option is presumed to be valued by the owner-manager at its market value. This is consistent with the original assumption that the owner manager considers the assets at market value in making production financing decisions. This is also in accord with the implication in Jensen-Meckling, "Theory of the Firm" (pp. 352–353), in which the owner-manager is bound to hold equity shares, but they are presumed to be valued at market. However, the analytical procedure in this chapter can easily account for any adjustments in market value, which reflect your welfare loss as manager, in determining the true value of the package of securities you are bound to hold. This is because, in accordance with Jensen and Meckling, it is assumed here that your utility function is known to the market.

[22] The reader is referred to Haugen and Senbet, "Resolving the Agency Problems," for a solution under more general conditions.

receipts from outsiders, must sum up to total firm value [the budget constraint]; (c) there exists no incentive for the manager to avoid value maximizing projects in preference for high- (low-) variance (but suboptimal) investment opportunities [the risk incentive constraint]. The objective is to solve for three variables that satisfy the preceding conditions. The three variables are: (a) the manager's fractional ownership interest in the firm (α); (b) the exercise price (E_c) for the call option retained by the manager; and (c) the exercise price (E_p) for the put option retained by external capital contributors.

As we show in the Appendix to this chapter, the solution is given by:

$$E_C = \frac{2\phi V^{*2} + R(V^* - V_s)}{2V^*}$$

$$E_P = \frac{2\phi V^{*2} - R(V^* - V_s)}{2V^*}$$

$$\alpha = \frac{(E_C - E_P)}{R}$$

where:

$$R = V_2 - V_1$$

$$\phi = 1/(1+r_f) = \text{the discount factor}$$

Consider the following example:

$$V^* = \$1000 \qquad R = \$800$$

$$\phi = 1 \qquad V_S = \$800$$

In this case the solution is given by:

$$\alpha - .2$$

$$E_C = 1{,}080$$

$$E_P = 920$$

Figure 6.4 depicts the terminal value of the package held by the outside financiers as a function of the ending value of the firm. The terminal value is given by $(1-\alpha)V + V_P - V_C = .8V + \max(920 - V, 0) - \max(V - 1{,}080, 0)$, and it is represented by the solid kinked function running along the top of the diagram. The uniform distribution for the terminal value of the firm is given by the rectangle centered on $V^* = \$1{,}000$. Given this distribution, we see that the expected (and in this case present market) value of the package is $800. As the entrepreneur increases or decreases his or her consumption of perquisites, this rectangle shifts to the left and to the

Figure 6.4. Simultaneous Resolution of Risk and Perk Incentive Problems with a Put and Call Option

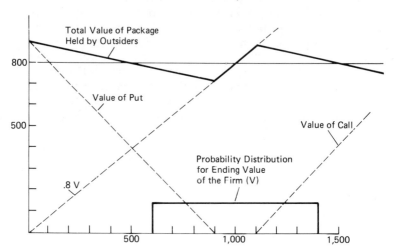

Package Held by Outsiders (Current Market Value = $800)

1. 80 percent of common stock
2. Positive position in a put option (E = $920)
3. Negative position in a call option (E = $1,080)

Package Held by Owner-Manager

1. 20 percent of common stock
2. Negative position in a put option (E = $920)
3. Positive position in a call option (E = $1,080)

right, respectively. Note that such a shift has no effect on the present market value of the financial package held by outsiders, for what they lose on one side of the distribution is always exactly offset by what they gain on the other. The value of the package is insensitive to perquisite consumption on the part of the entrepreneur. This means that the market value of the *entrepreneur's* package must fluctuate dollar for dollar with changes in the amount of perquisites consumed. The entrepreneur pays for perks in full as he or she would as sole owner.

Any change in the risk of the firm is reflected in a change in R, the difference between the highest and lowest possible terminal values for the firm. Note that, once again, increases or decreases in the range of possible terminal values have no effect on the expected terminal value of the package held by outsiders or its current market value. This means that the entrepreneur is unable to expropriate wealth from the outside financiers by changing the risk of the firm, if they hold this particular package of securities.

The package held by outsiders is obviously not riskless. Its *terminal* value fluctuates with the ending value of the firm. However, its *present* market value is insensitive to changes in the present market value of the firm and to changes in the variance of the firm's underlying assets. The risk and perk incentive problems are completely neutralized by issuing the package.[23]

In sum, a simultaneous solution to the perquisite consumption and risk incentive problems requires the coexistence of executive stock options and convertible debt. This constitutes a strong economic rationale for a complex capital structure that consists of straight equity, straight debt, and convertible debt. Straight equity is represented by stock options retained by an owner-executive. Straight debt is represented by the managerial ownership interest in the original equity, which is now essentially converted into risky debt due to the issuance of stock options. Convertible debt is represented by the combined positions of external financiers in the put and original equity. The capital structure can be made even more complex by attaching a call provision to the convertible debt, as is commonly done in actual practice. This is especially useful when there exists an agency problem of informational asymmetry. Such a complex capital structure plays a vital role in a simultaneous solution to the perk, risk incentive, and informational asymmetry problems. It is our view that call provisions attached to convertible debt are useful in resolving agency problems rather than enforcing conversion as it is commonly assumed in popular finance texts. The basic decision criterion to call a bond must remain the same as the one specified in Section 6.4 irrespective of whether or not the bond is convertible.

6.7 Further Complex Features

So far we have addressed the most popular complex features in financial contracts. In closing this chapter, we wish to make a brief

---

[23] Now recall the economic theory of agency discussed in Section 6.2. Our solution is "first-best" if you are risk neutral as an entrepreneur. However, you need not be risk neutral if you can identify another firm or portfolio of firms that is highly and positively correlated with your own firm. You can then reduce the risk associated with random fluctuations in your firm value by taking a short position in the other firm or portfolio. You can also use the proceeds, V_S, to further diversify your holdings. See R. Haugen and L. Senbet "Resolving the Agency Problems of External Capital Through Options" for a general solution. The standard economic theory of agency ignores market opportunities for risk reduction. On the other hand, neither our solution nor the original exposition by Jensen and Meckling (footnote 5, Chapter 3) *explicitly* addresses the costs associated with suboptimal risk sharing. However, even if the solutions are costly, they still rationalize the existence of complex capital structure as a means of mitigating certain classes of agency problems.

remark about two other complexities that exist in the financial world. Typically a bond indenture is complex. It specifies certain restrictions on the behavior of management working in the best interests of stockholders (agents). Agency problems associated with risk shifting, informational asymmetry, and forgone growth opportunities are controlled in part through indenture covenants that restrict the acquisition and disposition of certain assets and limit dividend payments. This direct route, which controls the dividend and investment policies of the firm, may be quite costly, especially when these optimal policies must be compromised in the future so as to meet indenture restrictions. It should again be recognized, though, that call provisions in corporate debt can mitigate agency costs associated with restrictive covenants.

The agency cost associated with bankruptcy may also call for the issuance of a complex debt instrument. The obvious analog of this complexity in the context of bankruptcy problems is the issuance of income bonds. Interest payments on these bonds are required only if earned. Income bonds can, however, trigger bankruptcy at maturity from the firm's failure to meet principal payments. Perpetual income bonds would seem to satisfy this deficiency, but even prior to maturity, income bonds can trigger technical default if available cash is incommensurate with current earnings and hence is insufficient to meet current interest payments. Income bonds are rarely issued by firms, possibly because (1) they are unable to fully resolve bankruptcy problems; and (2) natural market mechanisms are relatively efficient in resolving these problems. Unlike income bonds, interest on conventional coupon bonds is payable irrespective of the level of current earnings. Otherwise, default would occur. Since each coupon payment can be regarded as a bond, there is a higher probability of default with conventional bonds than income bonds. Income bonds can also be readily comparable with preferred stock, but, unlike the latter, they carry the "tax" benefit of interest payment deduction.

6.8 Conclusion

Agency problems that remain unresolved spontaneously through the market place can be mitigated through complex financial contracts. Such complex features as call provisions in corporate debt, conversion privileges, and executive stock options are capable of realigning the diverse interests of various classes of securityholders. In particular, such contracts are vital in resolving the agency problems of risk shifting, informational asymmetry, excessive managerial perquisite consumption, and foregone growth opportunities. We find that when these problems exist simultaneously, they call for the coexistence of various complex features in financial contracting. That is why a strong economic rationale is provided for the existence of observed complex capital structures consisting not only of straight debt and equity capital, but also convertible securities, callable debt, callable-convertible debt, and executive stock options. The next chapter examines the optimality of capital structure in the face of taxes and residual agency problems that still remain unresolved through either the market place or complex financial contracts.

Appendix: *An Illustration for the Zero Agency Cost Solution for a Particular Option Pricing Function*

WE shall illustrate a zero agency cost solution by using a particular pricing function for the call and put options. The solution must satisfy three conditions; a) you as manager consume no excess perquisites beyond what is optimal for the sole owner [the perk constraint]; b) your total wealth, including receipts from outsiders, must sum up to total firm value [the budget constraint]; c) there exists no incentive for you to avoid value maximizing projects in preference for high- (low-) variance (but suboptimal) investment opportunities [the risk incentive constraint]. The objective is to solve for three variables that satisfy the preceding conditions. The three variables are: a) your fractional ownership interest in the firm (α); b) the exercise price (E_C) for the call option retained by you; and c) the exercise price (E_P) for the put option retained by external capital contributors.

In deriving the pricing functions for the call and put, we employ two simplifying assumptions. First, the capital market is characterized by investors who are risk neutral, so that the expected return on all assets is equal to the riskless rate of interest. Second, the terminal value of the firm is uniformly distributed over the interval $[V_1, V_2]$, where V_2 is the limiting value in the uniform distribution. Thus, the values of the (European) call and put can be specified as:

$$V_C = \phi^{-1} \frac{1}{R} \int_{E_C}^{V_2} (X - E_c)\, dX = \frac{(V_2 - E_C)^2}{2\phi R} \qquad (A.1)$$

$$V_P = \phi^{-1} \frac{1}{R} \int_{V_1}^{E_P} (E_P - X)\, dX = \frac{(E_P - V_1)^2}{2\phi R} \qquad (A.2)$$

106

where

ϕ = one plus the riskless rate of interest
X = a variable of integration for the terminal value of the firm
$R = V_2 - V_1; \dfrac{1}{R}$ = the density function, which is constant for a uniform distribution

The options are assumed to be European-type with a single period to expiration.

The above relations in (A.1) and (A.2) obtain when E_C and E_P lie within the interval $[V_1, V_2]$. When the exercise prices lie outside the interval, the values of the call and the put collapse to:

$$V_C = \begin{cases} V - \phi^{-1} E_C & \text{if } E_C < V_1 \\ 0 & \text{if } E_C > V_2 \end{cases}$$

$$V_P = \begin{cases} 0 & \text{if } E_P < V_1 \\ \phi^{-1} E_P - V & \text{if } E_P > V_2 \end{cases}$$

where

$$V = \phi^{-1} \left[\frac{V_1 + V_2}{2} \right] = \text{the current value of the firm}$$

Thus, exercise prices outside the interval imply either worthless options or options that are sure to be exercised. However, neither of these are feasible for the zero agency cost solution. For instance, a call option to buy back the entire firm at a specific price, which is sure to be exercised, implies that the external capital is completely riskless, and there exists no agency problem with riskless external financing. Hereafter, we seek solutions that lead to the exercise prices that lie in the interval $[V_1, V_2]$, and hence we utilize the expressions in (A.1) and (A.2) for our analytical framework.

It is instructive to recast the call and put option values in terms of V, the current value of the firm, so that

$$V_C = \frac{(\phi V + R/2 - E_C)^2}{2\phi R} \tag{A.3}$$

$$V_P = \frac{(E_P + R/2 - \phi V)^2}{2\phi R} \tag{A.4}$$

In deriving (A.3) and (A.4) we have employed the fact that $R = V_2 - V_1 = 2(\phi V - V_1)$. The sensitivity of the option values with respect to the underlying value (V) can be expressed as

$$\frac{\partial V_C}{\partial V} = \frac{2\phi V + R - 2E_C}{2R} \tag{A.5}$$

$$\frac{\partial V_P}{\partial V} = \frac{2\phi V - R - 2E_P}{2R} \tag{A.6}$$

Given that E_C and E_P lie within the interval $[V_1, V_2]$, it is easily seen that V_C is an increasing function of V, while V_P is a decreasing function of V. Indeed, the RHS of (A.5) collapses to $(V_2 - E_C)/R$, which is a positive quantity, whereas the RHS of (A.6) is $(V_1 - E_P)/R$, a negative amount. We shall employ these expressions interchangeably in subsequent analysis. Note also that (A-5), or alternatively $(V_2 - E_C)/R$, is the *probability* of exercising the call option.

Similarly, we can express the sensitivity of the option values with respect to variance or standard deviation. The variance of the uniform variable in this case is $R^2/12$, which is merely the square of the range scaled by a constant. Consequently, without loss of generality, we employ R^2 or R as an index of dispersion. Thus, the sensitivity can be expressed as

$$\frac{\partial V_C}{\partial R} = \frac{1}{2\phi R^2}(R/2 + A)(R/2 - A) = \frac{R^2 - 4A^2}{8\phi R^2} \tag{A.7}$$

$$\frac{\partial V_P}{\partial R} = \frac{1}{2\phi R^2}(R/2 + D)(R/2 - D) = \frac{R^2 - 4D^2}{8\phi R^2} \tag{A.8}$$

where

$$A = \phi V - E_C$$

$$D = \phi V - E_P$$

Again it can be shown that (A.7) and (A.8) are both positive, given that E_C and E_P lie in the interval $[V_1, V_2]$.[1] Therefore, as expected, the values of the call and the put are increasing functions of R.

We can now express the constraints underlying the zero agency cost solution in terms of the specific option pricing functions derived above.

---

[1] Alternative expressions exist for (A.7) and (A.8) such that

$$\frac{\partial V_C}{\partial R} = \frac{(V_2 - E_C)(E_C - V_1)}{2\phi R^2} > 0 \tag{A.7'}$$

and

$$\frac{\partial V_P}{\partial R} = \frac{(E_P - V_1)(V_2 - E_P)}{2\phi R^2} > 0 \tag{A.8'}$$

These alternatives are employed in subsequent analysis whenever useful.

The Perk Constraint

$$\alpha + \left.\frac{\partial V_C}{\partial V}\right|_{V^*} - \left.\frac{\partial V_P}{\partial V}\right|_{V^*} = \alpha + \frac{(V_2 - E_C)}{R} - \frac{(V_1 - E_P)}{R} = 1 \quad (A.9)$$

where

the partials are evaluated at $V^* = \overline{V} - F^* =$ the total firm value at the zero agency cost solution. For our purpose, $V^* = (V_1 + V_2)/2\phi$.

The perk constraint is intended to ensure that you as manager consume no excess perquisites. In other words, the cost to you of consuming a dollar of perks is entirely borne by you in the form of a commensurate change in your wealth (V_W), at a utility maximizing point (V^*, F^*) in Figure 6.3. The second order condition will depend on your utility function, and we assume that the condition is satisfied.

The Budget Constraint

$$V_W = V_S + \alpha V^* + V_C(V^*) - V_P(V^*) = V^*$$

or

$$V_S + V^*(\alpha - 1)$$

$$+ \frac{(\phi V^* + R/2 - E_C)^2 - (E_P + R/2 - \phi V^*)^2}{2\phi R} = 0 \quad (A.10)$$

The managerial wealth, including receipts from external security-holders, must sum up to total firm value, V^*, at the zero agency cost solution. Notice that the options are evaluated at V^*.

The Risk Incentive Constraint

The call option retained by you as owner-manager creates an incentive for you to shift to high risk (and possibly suboptimal) investment opportunities. On the other hand, the put option retained by outside capital contributors creates a countervailing risk incentive. We wish to specify a constraint, so that the marginal wealth changes due to changes in the call and put option values is zero when you shift to an unwarranted risk. We assume that the investment opportunity set available to you as the entrepreneur is known to the market. This set can be mapped into its corresponding risk (R), so that we can specify the value of an investment opportunity as $V = f(R)$. There exists no cause and effect relationship between V and R, but we assume, for simplicity, a continuum of project values and their corresponding risks. Assume that the investment opportunities are arranged in an increasing order of R. If the manager shifts to an unwarranted risk, the option values change not only due to the change in R, but also due to the change in V. Thus, we can express the risk incentive constraint as:

$$\frac{dZ}{dR} = \frac{\partial V_C}{\partial V} f'(R) + \frac{\partial V_C}{\partial R} - \frac{\partial V_P}{\partial V} f'(R) + \frac{\partial V_P}{\partial R} = 0$$

where

$$Z = V_C [f(R), R] - V_P [f(R), R]$$

Invoking all the results in (A.5) up to (A.8) and evaluating them at V*, we obtain the risk incentive constraint in the following simplified form:

$$(E_C^2 - E_P^2) + 2(E_P - F_C)[\phi V^* - \phi R f'(R)] - 2\phi R^2 f'(R) = 0 \quad (A.11)$$

For purposes of checking the second order condition, we establish the following expression after considerable simplification of partials and cross partials

$$\frac{d^2 Z}{dR^2} = \frac{2}{R^2}(E_C - E_P)f'(R) + \frac{(E_P - E_C + R)}{R}f''(R) + \frac{(A^2 - D^2)}{\phi R^3} \quad (A.12)$$

As we shall see later, the second order condition is satisfied. (See footnote 2.)

The Zero Agency Cost Solution

Now we have a system of three equations [(A.9), (A.10), and (A.11)] in the three unknowns E_C, E_P, and α. The amount of external financing needed by the entrepreneur (V_S) is fixed. We solve for α from (A.9) as

$$\alpha = \frac{(E_C - E_P)}{R} \quad (A.13)$$

Substituting (A.13) for α in (A.10), we combine the perk and the budget constraints, and simplify the combined expression to arrive at

$$\left(E_P^2 - E_C^2\right) + R(E_C + E_P) - 2\phi R V_S = 0 \quad (A.14)$$

Now we have a system of two quadratic equations, (A.14) and (A.11), in the two unknowns, E_C and E_P. Before we proceed with our solution, we wish to argue that the option contract must be designed so as to force the entrepreneur to adopt a value maximizing strategy. Along a continuum of projects in the function $V = f(R)$, V is maximized when $f'(R) = 0$ and $f''(R) < 0$. Given this rationale, (A.11) collapses to

$$(E_C - E_P)(E_C + E_P - 2\phi V^*) = 0 \quad (A.15)$$

Two conditions satisfy (A.15), namely

$$\text{a) } E_C = E_P$$

$$\text{b) } E_C + E_P = 2\phi V^*$$

The first condition is unacceptable, because it implies that you as manager surrender all your ownership interests [see (A.13)] by retaining a package that includes a positive position in the call option and a negative position in the put option with identical parameters as the call. This combined position is equivalent to holding an option which is sure to be exercised. Under this condition we can solve for $E_C = E_P = \phi V_S$ from (A.14), implying that the net value of the assets held by you as manager is $V^* - V_S$. Notice that with the option contract, the original equity is essentially converted into debt so that, in this case, the manager holds a 100 percent of "equity" (option). Since the option is sure to be exercised, it must mean that debt is riskless. Thus, the first condition satisfying (A.15) sterilizes the agency problem of external financing. Consequently, we find condition (a) unacceptable.

We can now move to condition (b) and use it along with (A.14) to solve for E_C and E_P. Thus,

$$E_C = \frac{2\phi V^{*2} + R(V^* - V_S)}{2V^*} \tag{A.16}$$

$$E_P = \frac{2\phi V^{*2} - R(V^* - V_S)}{2V^*} \tag{A.17}$$

Now (A.13), (A.16), and (A.17) constitute the zero agency cost solution. Under this solution, you as manager retain a positive fractional interest (α), because $E_C > E_P$, as we see from (A.16) and (A.17). Indeed, the RHS of (A.14) is equivalent to $(1 - V_S/V^*)$. This in turn implies that the option contract must be designed so as to equate the values of the call and the put. Since the positions in the options cancel out in terms of current value, we can say that the original equity has not been transformed into debt as previously expected. Its form remains intact.[2]

---

[2] The second-order condition for the risk incentive constraint can be checked from (A.12). As we argued earlier, $f'(R)$ is zero at the solution point. Thus, we ignore the first term of the RHS of (A.12) and concentrate on the two subsequent terms. The second term is equivalent to $(1 + \alpha)f''(R)$ [see eq. (A.13) and hence negative since $f''(R)$ is negative at the solution point. Also, it is easy to see that the last term of the RHS is negative, since $E_C > E_P$ in our solution. Consequently, the entire expression in (A.12) is negative, and the second-order condition is, thus, satisfied for the risk incentive constraint.

```
7777777777777777777777777777777777777777777777777777777777777777777777777777777777777777
7777777777777777777777777777777777777777777777777777777777777777777777777777777777777777
7777777777777777777777777777    77777777777   777    777    7777777777777777777777777777
7777777777777777777777777777    777777777    7777    777    7777777777777777777777777777
77777777777777777777777777777    77777777    77777    777    777777777777777777777777777
777777777777777777777777777777    777777    777777    777    777777777777777777777777777
7777777777777777777777777777777    77777    7777777    777    77777777777777777777777777
77777777777777777777777777777777    777    7777777    777    777777777777777777777777777
777777777777777777777777777777777    7    777777777    777    77777777777777777777777777
7777777777777777777777777777777777        777777777    777    77777777777777777777777777
77777777777777777777777777777777777    777777777    777    777777777777777777777777777777
7777777777777777777777777777777777777777777777777777777777777777777777777777777777777777
7777777777777777777777777777777777777777777777777777777777777777777777777777777777777777
```

Agency Problems and the Relative Pricing
of Financial Securities

7.1 Introduction

THE Miller bond market equilibrium analysis, which was presented in detail in Chapter 2, provides important insights into the determinants of corporate bond yields. In particular, Miller shows that corporate bonds are priced to yield a tax premium that fully reflects the *corporate tax rate*. This is a rather surprising result. Previous literature on the pricing of taxable corporate bonds largely focused on the marginal tax rates of *investors* to explain the yield differential between taxable and tax exempt securities. Determination of bond prices (yields) by demand alone implies that corporations, which supply bonds, do not respond by adjusting supplies in response to observed yield differentials. The Miller analysis, on the other hand, considers both the demand and the supply of bonds. Firms, which observe the tax savings property of debt, finance exclusively with debt (and make a "supply adjustment") as long as the tax premium in the cost of debt is below that implied by the corporate tax rate. By the same token, they will avoid debt completely if the premium is above that implied by the corporate tax rate. Equilibrium can be reached only if the (risk adjusted) yield on corporate bonds includes a tax premium that exactly and fully incorporates the corporate tax rate.[1] Thus, if the applicable

---

[1] As was shown in Chapter 2, the Miller analysis predicts that for a given certainty equivalent return on equity (r*), the equilibrium yield on a taxable corporate bond

tax rate is 50 percent (federal and state) the risk adjusted expected return on taxable corporate bonds will be twice as high as the risk adjusted expected return on common stock (if the income from stock can be costlessly tax sheltered) or tax exempt bonds.

A bond interest rate, which is consistent with the Miller analysis, includes the following components, which add up to the promised bond yield:[2]

- the risk free tax exempt rate
- a default premium
- a risk premium
- a tax premium based on the corporate tax rate

The reader should recall from Chapter 2 the significance of the exact magnitude of the tax premium. If the tax premium is exactly that implied by the corporate tax rate, individual firms face the capital structure decision with indifference. Thus, a tax induced yield differential that exactly reflects the corporate tax rate and the irrelevance of the capital structure decision are two interrelated predictions of the Miller analysis.

Although the evidence on this issue has been inconsistent, some empirical studies of the tax rate embedded in yield differential show that the rate is significantly lower than the corporate tax rate. Moreover, real world, publicly held corporations engage in active management of capital structure. The seeming relevancy of the capital structure decision in observed corporate behavior, coupled with evidence of a lower than expected tax premium and variation in the tax premium over time when the corporate tax rate remained constant, is inconsistent with the Miller analysis.[3]

The apparent difficulties in verifying the predictions of the Miller

---

must be given by $r^*/(1 - \tau_c)$, where τ_c is the corporate tax rate. Hence, tax induced yield differentials in the magnitude of $\Delta = r^*/(-\tau_c) - r^* = r^*\tau_c/(1-\tau_c)$ are expected to characterize the pricing of taxable versus nontaxable financial instruments.

[2] The terms "yield" and "return" are used interchangeably in this chapter. This is consistent with a one period discount bond. For multiperiod bonds, our analysis focuses on holding period returns or the return achieved in terms of interest income and capital gains by buying a bond at the beginning of a period and selling it at the end of the period. The distribution of holding period returns is required to price stocks and bonds in an integrated capital market.

[3] As was shown in Chapter 2, the Miller analysis predicts that investors will sort themselves into tax induced "leverage clienteles." Wealthy investors, for example, prefer to invest in firms with low leverage. They achieve superior after tax portfolio performance by engaging in personal borrowing that takes advantage of interest deductions based on their (high) marginal taxes. The search for these tax induced clienteles in actual investment portfolios has not produced any meaningful association between the leverage of companies included in the portfolios of particular investors and measures of the same investors' marginal tax rates. Thus, another prediction of the analysis seems to be inconsistent with observed behavior of investors.

analysis call for modifications in the analysis, taking into account certain market imperfections that may be responsible for the observed corporate behavior. This point should be further clarified. Miller considers market imperfections, such as discriminatory corporate taxes that allow for the deduction of interest payments but not dividend payments. But this type of imperfection is not unique to any particular firm. All firms face the same tax subsidy of debt (as all interest is assumed to be deductible against a single corporate tax rate) and all become indifferent to debt financing when the yield "grosses up" this tax subsidy. Other imperfections impact unevenly on different firms. As these imperfections modify the supply of bonds by individual firms, we call them "supply side modifications." Two types of modifications are considered. First, we allow for a differential tax subsidy of debt across firms. This is achieved by assuming that each firm has a different amount of non-debt related tax deductions, such as depreciation or investment tax credits. The availability of non-debt related deductions affects the value of debt as a source of tax savings. As more non-debt related deductions are present for a particular firm, the possibility increases that interest expenses will be redundant. This diminishes the expected value of the tax subsidy associated with successive units of debt issued, and also diminishes the incentive to issue debt.[4] Second, we allow for firm specific agency costs of debt.[5] Firms facing those costs are expected to limit their supply of debt as the tax subsidy may be more than offset by the magnitude of the (marginal) agency costs of debt.

Completing the two supply side modifications, we turn to the demand curve in the Miller analysis. Chapter 2 explained in detail the construction of the demand curve based on the progression of marginal personal taxes. It was assumed then that investors face the full tax consequences of receiving interest income. This assumption is replaced by allowing investors to use tax shelters, which provide limited forms of tax avoidance.

Utilization of tax shelters by individuals is obviously an observable phenomenon. The fact that the same individual still pays some taxes implies that sheltering income is in some sense costly. These costs may be direct, such as charges imposed by an intermediary whose service is required to obtain the tax shelter,[6] or they may be indirect, such as implicit costs imposed on an individual who decides to deviate from an otherwise optimal portfolio composition in order to invest in tax

---

[4] The analysis of non-debt related tax shields draws on H. DeAngelo and R. Masulis, "Optimal Capital Structure Under Corporate and Personal Taxation," *Journal of Financial Economics* (March 1980).

[5] Chapter 3 explains in detail the emergence and nature of agency costs of debt.

[6] In M. Miller & M. Scholes, "Dividends and Taxes," *Journal of Financial Economics* (March 1978), investors obtain (interest) tax deductions by borrowing money to invest in tax free annuities supplied by insurance companies.

sheltered assets. The equilibrium that emerges after introducing these modifications is consistent with (a) optimal capital structure for the single firm, (b) pricing of taxable securities at a tax rate that is below the corporate rate, and (c) the existence of complex securities that are issued to (partially) resolve firm-specific agency problems.

7.2 Motivation for Generalizing the Miller Equilibrium

In the Miller analysis, the equilibrium yield differential on taxable corporate bonds is given by $\Delta = r^* \tau_c/(1 - \tau_c)$. Given $r^* = 10\%$ and $\tau_c = 50\%$, $\Delta = 10\%$, and hence a 10% yield differential exists between taxable and nontaxable financial instruments having the same level of investment risk. An immediate issue is the empirical verification of this prediction. An empirical test of tax induced yield differentials seems to be an easy task. This view is misleading. To construct such a test, one has to make adjustments for at least three sets of factors. First, one has to adjust for risk, which in turn requires a prespecified valuation model, such as the capital asset pricing model. Obviously, once a particular valuation model is employed, the results of the test are conditional upon this choice. Second, one has to adjust for various features of bond contracts, such as sinking funds, callability, and quality of borrower (see Chapter 4), which is particularly difficult because the existence of call features or sinking fund provisions determines the maturity of the bond.[7] Third, one has to consider the uncertainties of differential tax status resulting from potential legislative changes by Congress; for example, one must consider the tax exempt status of municipal bonds or the tax deferred status of dividends paid on public utility shares.

Estimates of the tax rates that are embedded in risk adjusted yield differentials between bonds with differing tax exposure were obtained by McCulloch and Skelton.[8] The rate estimate obtained by McCulloch was considerably less than the corporate rate. While Skelton obtained a rate estimate that was not significantly different from the corporate tax rate for short term municipals, his rate estimate for long term bonds was significantly less than 48 percent plus the applicable state tax.

Tests on the existence of leverage clienteles were conducted by Kim, et al.[9] The tests were based on the association between the financial leverage of companies that are included in investors' stock portfolios

---

[7] It should be noted that almost all corporate bonds include a call provision, while the bulk of government bonds are not callable.

[8] See J. McCulloch, "The Tax-Adjusted Yield Curve," *Journal of Finance* (June 1975) and J. Skelton, "The Relative Pricing of Tax-Exempt and Taxable Debt," Working Paper, University of California, Berkeley.

[9] E. Kim, W. LeWellen, and J. McConnell, "Financial Leverage Clienteles: Theory and Evidence," *Journal of Financial Economics* (March 1979).

and the tax brackets of these investors. Data on the composition of actual stock portfolios were obtained from brokerage houses. Tax brackets were estimated using proxies for earned income. The study was not able to detect any meaningful association between these variables so that the prediction on the existence of leverage clienteles is not supported by actual data.[10]

Miller suggests that, in equilibrium, financial leverage is a matter of indifference to individual corporations. This follows as the (equilibrium) prices of taxable corporate bonds "gross up" the *entire* tax advantage of debt financing at the corporate level. The "gain from leverage" disappears altogether and we are back in an environment in which the value of the levered firm is identical to the value of the unlevered firm, even in the presence of taxes.

Direct tests of the irrelevancy of corporate capital structure are difficult to construct (see Modigliani and Miller (1966)). Casual observation indicates that complex capital structures exist. We not only see cross-sectional variations in debt-to-equity ratios, which relate systematically to type of industry, but also a multiplicity of maturity structures, call and conversion features, various types of covenants, redemption arrangements, etc. It appears that the characteristics of corporate debt are not chosen at random as particular debt characteristics are peculiar to particular industries. While it is difficult to accept the consistency of these observations with the proposition that capital structure is irrelevant, we must still provide direct evidence on the link between financial policies and market values. Robert Litzenberger views the empirical evidence regarding the effect of the capital structure on the value of the firm as indicating that, at least in some cases, there appears to be a direct causational link between the two variables.[11] Both Sosin and Masulis, in their independent studies, find evidence that the market values of firms are sensitive to the financing mix in certain cases, such as stock repurchases and pure financial recapitalizations.[12] Such evidence is obviously not in line with the prediction of the Miller equilibrium.

7.3 Generalizations of the Miller Analysis

In this section, two crucial restrictions of the Miller analysis are reexamined. On the supply side, we consider the possibility that the nature of the firms' assets and future investment opportunities may

---

[10] It should be noted, however, that the scope of this empirical study is severely limited by the lack of reliable measures of marginal tax rates.

[11] R. Litzenberger, "Debt, Taxes and Incompleteness: A Survey," Unpublished manuscript, Stanford University.

[12] See R. Masulis, "The Effects of Capital Structure Changes on Security Prices: A Study of Exchange Offers," *Journal of Financial Economics* (June 1980) and H. Sosin, "Neutral Recapitalizations: Predictions and Tests Concerning Valuation and Welfare," *Journal of Finance* (September 1978).

affect their supply of debt. Corporations issue debt to obtain an interest deduction. Under the Miller analysis, this deduction is certain
and constant per unit of debt issued (see Chapter 2). In reality, however, firms may vary in their ability to utilize interest deductions.
DeAngelo and Masulis (1980) suggest that the existence of non-debt
related tax shields, such as depreciation charges, may make the interest deduction redundant in states of nature where the return on
assets is low relative to the depreciation deduction.[13] In addition to
taking account of non-debt related tax deductions, the Miller analysis
is modified by introducing agency problems, which tend to limit the
supply of debt and produce an equilibrium in which firms are no
longer indifferent to the capital structure decision.

On the demand side, Miller assumes that investors are subject to
the full burden of personal taxes on their interest income. In reality,
however, investors engage in many forms of tax arbitrage, thereby
moderating their exposure to income tax on investment income. Miller
and Scholes suggest a tax planning strategy that eliminates the tax
exposure of dividend income.[14] Obviously, similar tax arbitrage strategies can be applied to interest income. Nonetheless, we observe that
investors pay taxes. This suggests that tax avoidance is costly. Allowing
for (costly) tax avoidance affects the shape of the demand curve for
corporate bonds by making it more elastic.

These modifications in the Miller analysis produce equilibrium prices
for bonds in which the tax induced yield differential is lower than
the differential predicted by Miller. Optimal capital structure for the
single firm is obtained where the amount of debt is inversely related
to (1) the availability of non-debt related tax shields, and (2) the magnitude of (marginal) agency costs of debt.

7.31 Determinants of the Tax Subsidy of Debt for the Individual Firm

The emphasis on the tax advantage of debt financing is taken from
the seminal contribution of Modigliani and Miller (1963; see Chapter
2). Assuming a perpetual nongrowing firm and riskless debt, MM
derive the value of the tax subsidy (see Chapter 2) as a linear function
of the amount of debt employed. The same structure is utilized by
Miller, who develops his analysis of bond market equilibrium in the
context of a constant tax subsidy per unit of debt. This, in turn,
justifies the perfectly elastic supply schedule for debt financing for
the individual firm. Several recent papers modify the tax assumptions
of Miller.

DeAngelo and Masulis[15] extend the analysis of Miller by considering

---

[13] H. DeAngelo and R. Masulis, "Optimal Capital Structure Under Corporate and
Personal Taxation," *Journal of Financial Economics* (March 1980).

[14] R. Dammon, "Portfolio Selection, Capital Structure, and Taxes," Wisconsin Working Paper (April 1984). See footnote 26.

[15] H. DeAngelo and R. Masulis, *ibid.*

the effect of non-debt related tax shields on the supply curve of corporate bonds. Non-debt related tax shields are non-cash tax deductions, such as accounting depreciation, depletion allowances, and the investment tax credit. Full utilization of these deductions for tax purposes depends on the magnitude of taxable income. As more debt is introduced into the capital structure, and consequently as more interest expenses are claimed against taxable income, the probability of full utilization of alternative tax shields diminishes.

The analysis explicitly assumes that markets for tax shelters are imperfect, as the tax authorities prohibit the unlimited sale or purchase of tax deductions. Carrybacks and carryforwards of losses for tax purposes are also limited.[16] Under these two assumptions, unutilized deductions are lost so that additional interest expenses called for by an increase in the amount of debt may be redundant. Consequently, the value of the tax subsidy that is associated with debt financing declines at the margin.[17] The supply curve for corporate debt is no longer horizontal at the rate $r^*/(1 - \tau)$ as lower interest rates are required to entice firms to issue more debt. DeAngelo and Masulis demonstrate that interior optimal capital structures exist for individual firms under certain assumptions. Firms having access to large quantities of non-debt related tax shields issue small amounts of debt, and firms that have access to small quantitites of these shields rely more heavily on debt financing to shelter their taxable income.

DeAngelo and Masulis' analysis is based on an explicit assumption that carryback and carryforward of losses are disallowed. Stated differently, they assume that the value of nonutilized deductions (e.g., losses for tax purposes) is zero. Under this assumption, they are able to generate a downward sloping supply curve for corporate debt and an optimal debt to equity ratio for the individual firm. To put this assumption in perspective, one has to note that, even in a multiperiod context where carrybacks and carryforwards are possible, the mechanism that allows for their utilization is not perfect. The firm not only loses the time value of money, but there are limitations on the period of carryovers, and the transfer of losses to other firms via mergers or takeovers is costly.

Finally, we note that the value of tax subsidy of debt depends on the time pattern of taxable income that is produced by the firms' assets.[18] In most of the literature the cash flows are assumed to be

---

[16] The tax code sets limitations on the use of carrybacks and carryforwards. Generally, carrybacks are limited to three years and carryforwards to five years. No compensation is given for the deferral of utilizing past deductions in future periods.

[17] This is obtained under an additional assumption that the principal and interest are deductible for tax purposes. The conclusion regarding the decline in the marginal tax subsidy of debt depends completely on the above assumptions.

[18] See also S. Myers, "Interactions of Corporate Financing and Investment Decisions—Implications for Capital Budgeting," *Journal of Finance* (March 1977).

perpetual. This assumption is explicit in MM and implicit in all studies which assume that principal as well as interest is tax deductible.[19] But if the cash flows vary in time, and recalling that the mechanism of carryovers is not perfect, the value of the tax subsidy of debt diminishes.[20] For example, consider two firms that have the same market value in a taxless world but one receives all its income immediately while the other receives a perpetual stream. Debt cannot shelter the income of the first firm as the interest deduction will be small for the short period of time until income is taxed. Debt can shelter completely the income of the second firm. Obviously, the value of the tax subsidy will be much higher for the second firm. It follows that situations of uneven cash flows over time, stochastically unstable cash flows, and shorter duration cash flows produce lower tax subsidy of debt. Firms for which those characteristics of asset cash flows are present will limit their supply of debt as the rate of interest on debt is increased. This is represented by a downward sloping supply curve such as ZYX in Figure 7.2 below.

7.32 Agency Costs of Debt

The nature of agency costs of debt has been detailed in Chapters 3 and 4. There we discussed the conditions under which agency costs of debt may be an increasing function of the amount of debt employed in the capital structure. Figure 7.1 plots the agency costs associated with a marginal unit of debt for an individual firm as a function of the amount of debt in the capital structure, assuming that the agency costs of equity are negligible. To simplify the graphical representation of the supply curve, but without loss of generality, we assume that the relationship is linear. The investment *opportunity set* is assumed to be given so that any increase in the amount of debt will increase the agency costs arising from the agency problems discussed above.

The supply curve for corporate bonds is depicted in Figure 7.2. Suppose that there are no limitations on the utilization of interest as a deductible expense so that each unit of debt produces a constant periodic tax saving of $\tau_c r$. In the *absence* of agency problems, corporations are indifferent between equity financing and debt financing so long as corporate debt yields the certainty-equivalent rate of interest $r^*/(1 - \tau_c)$. The horizontal supply curve in Figure 7.2 depicts this. If

---

[19] Deduction of principal in a single period analysis is equivalent, in present value, to the deduction of a perpetual stream of interest expenditures. For instance, see A. Kraus and R. Litzenberger, "A State-Preference Model of Optimal Capital Structure," *Journal of Finance* (September 1973) and DeAngelo and Masulis, *ibid.*

[20] F. Modigliani, "Debt, Dividend Policy, Taxes, Inflation and Market Valuation," *Journal of Finance* (May 1982) considers the tax subsidy of debt as a risky cash flow that should be discounted by the cost of capital and not by the risk-free rate. This modification affects the willingness of firms to issue debt at the rate $r^*/(1 - \tau_c)$.

Figure 7.1. Agency Costs and Debt

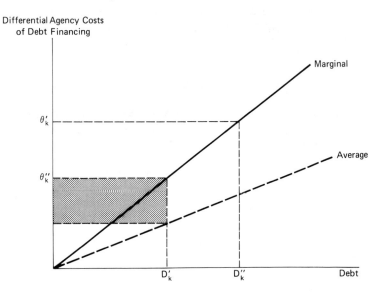

Figure 7.2. Bond Market Equilibrium with Costs of Agency Problems and Tax Avoidance

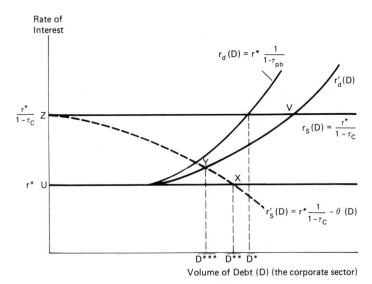

firms face agency costs, they are no longer indifferent between equity and debt financing when corporate debt yields $r^*/(1-\tau_c)$.[21] Nonetheless, they can be enticed into debt financing if the sum of the rate of interest on corporate bonds and the marginal agency cost as a percent of marginal debt financed, $\theta_k(D)$, is at most equal to $r^*/(1-\tau_c)$. Otherwise, debt financing is a losing proposition. Thus, in the presence of agency costs that increase at the margin, the supply curve is downward sloping as depicted by the schedule XYZ.

To see this, suppose that the certainty equivalent rate on corporate debt is $r' = r^*/(1-\tau_c) - \theta'$. It pays the individual firm to issue debt until the differential agency costs of debt financing $\theta_k(D)$ are equal to θ' for the marginal unit of debt. Thus, r' will be associated with a finite aggregate supply of debt across all firms in the economy. At a lower rate, it pays each firm to issue more debt so that aggregate supply is increased. Every point on the curve represents the quantity of bonds supplied as firms optimize their capital structures. In other words, the locus of points on the curve reflects corporate bond supply given that firms have achieved their (optimal) capital structure positions. As the interest rate on corporate debt falls, there is a general increase across all firms in the optimal amount of debt in capital structures.

While in general the tax subsidy rationale and the agency cost rationale may coexist, we find the agency cost rationale to be more interesting. Our reasoning for this statement is as follows. First, the agency cost rationale is richer in explaining not only the existence of debt but also its associated complexities, such as call provisions and conversion privileges, as was demonstrated in Chapter 6. Second, the agency rationale does not depend on particular tax assumptions, such as the prohibition of carryovers and the deduction of interest in bankruptcies. As was shown in the literature, the solution of the capital structure problem crucially depends on the tax assumptions used. Any departure from the perpetual riskless debt world of MM that causes changes in the underlying tax assumptions (e.g., an analysis of the tax subsidy in bankruptcy) may lead to a corner solution in which the firm finances all its assets by either debt or equity.[22]

Finally, we note that testing for the solution of the agency rationale versus, say, the tax subsidy rationale is difficult since both theories provide similar predictions on tax induced yield differentials. Also, consideration of duration and riskiness of assets in the context of the tax subsidy argument may create a severe identification problem since it is very likely that the same firms will also face severe agency problems.

---

[21] The analysis assumes away the effect of agency costs on equity. See Chapter 4 for the derivation of the trade-off between the two types of agency costs from which a rising marginal agency cost function of debt is obtained.

[22] This conclusion stands in contrast to DeAngelo and Masulis' conclusions.

7.33 Costly Tax Arbitrage for Individual Investors

In this section, we consider the effects of an explicit cost-of-tax-avoidance function on the demand for corporate bonds.[23] The ability of investors to engage in tax arbitrage is recognized in the literature. In some studies (e.g., Miller and Scholes), investors are allowed to engage costlessly in tax arbitrage up to the level of their investment income; however, no "spillover" of investment expense is allowed against other income. Obviously, tax arbitrage is prohibited in all studies that assume exogenous marginal tax rates for individual investors. Such an assumption seems to be inconsistent with the wide variety of possibilities for reducing tax liabilities—and marginal tax rates—by choosing particular mixtures of assets and liabilities that allow for front-end deduction of interest with tax deferral of income. Real estate investment financed by borrowing is one example of those possibilities.[24] The analysis is conducted under the assumption that investment strategies which save taxes exist but are costly to the investor. The costs of tax avoidance are both explicit (e.g., costs associated with financial intermediation or costs associated with shortselling) and implicit (e.g., costs associated with suboptimal portfolio diversification), and include the agency costs of *personal* debt financing required for tax avoidance. These costs, together with legal restrictions on some combinations of assets and liabilities, are taken into account in the process of investor portfolio optimization.

The dollar amount of the costs involved in tax avoidance is assumed to increase with the amount of tax sheltered income utilized by the investor. Two arguments justify this assumption. First, utilization of tax shelters forces the investors to deviate from utility maximizing optimal portfolios, which they would choose in the absence of taxes. Secondly, even in the absence of portfolio considerations, the tax code may prohibit excessive use of any given tax shelter, thus forcing investors to utilize alternative tax shelters which, at the margin, yield progressively lower returns. Also, if tax arbitrage involves the expedient of borrowing and lending simultaneously, the cost of financial inter-

---

[23] Obviously, tax arbitrage may also take place on the part of firms as well as investors. However, in order to simplify the analysis we have ignored the effects of tax avoidance at the corporate level.

[24] Miller and Scholes, *ibid.*, provide a detailed description of the tax provisions on the deductibility of interest and the tax treatment of income derived from selected tax shelters. To the tax shelters mentioned, we add the possibility of selling short high-dividend-paying stocks and purchasing equal-risk low-dividend-paying stocks. This will serve as a tax shelter since dividends are recognized as a front-end expense. As a general comment we add that tax provisions that allow for tax arbitrage are not strictly necessary to support models that predict the implications of tax arbitrage on security prices. Even if, by interpretation, tax provisions prohibit some combinations of assets and liabilities, it is effective enforcement of those laws, and the perceived penalties, which determine the utilization of those combinations by investors and their effect on observed market prices.

mediation would occur in the form of differential borrowing and lending rates. This cost is obviously an increasing function of leverage utilized in the tax arbitrage.

How would investors determine the amount of taxable corporate bonds in their portfolios? The solution must be based on the after (personal) tax return on all available investments. After-tax-returns obviously depend on the costs of tax avoidance, which may vary across different investments. So the inputs that are required to solve a portfolio selection problem are the parameters (means, variances, and covariances) of the after tax return distribution on all available assets. Minimizing the variances of portfolios of assets (for a given mean after tax return) produces an efficient frontier from which investors pick an (optimal) portfolio that includes an optimal amount invested in taxable corporate bonds. The demand curve in Figure 7.2 results from these optimizing decisions and, since it depends on the costs of tax avoidance, does not bear any *direct* relationship to a progression of marginal tax rates.

Increasing costs of tax avoidance are sufficient to generate the upward sloping demand curve for taxable corporate bonds. Note that because of the opportunity to avoid taxes (albeit at a cost) the demand curve exhibits greater elasticity than does Miller's. Moreover, unlike Miller's model, the upward sloping nature of the curve no longer reflects investors in progressively higher tax brackets. It merely reflects increasing aggregate demand by all investors in different tax brackets enticed by the increasing differential in yields on corporate bonds and tax exempt securities.

7.4 Tax-Induced Equilibrium Pricing of Financial Securities

Suppose that investors are able to arbitrage away costlessly all the tax implications of interest income, using the methods suggested by Miller and Scholes. The demand for corporate bonds is flat and the bond market equilibrium obtains when all securities, namely taxable bonds, tax-exempt bonds, and equity securities, yield the same certainty equivalent rate of return, r^*. This equilibrium is represented in Figure 7.2 by the point X at which the supply and demand for bonds is equal to D^{**} and the interest rate is $r(D^{**}) = r^*$. In this equilibrium, each firm provides a different amount of bonds. The amount is determined by its agency cost function satisfying $r^*/(1 - \tau_c) - r(D^{**}) = \theta_k(D_k) = \theta(D^{**})$. While the *marginal* agency costs are the same for all firms [and equal to the differential between the "grossed up" yield $r^*/(1 - \tau_c)$ and the final equilibrium yield $r(D^{**})$], the amount of debt that is issued to obtain this marginal agency cost, differs according to the firm specific cost function. Note that there are no *tax induced* differential returns in this equilibrium as investors are assumed to be able to eliminate costlessly the tax consequences of obtaining interest income. Obviously, such a conclusion is not supported by observable data as the existence of tax induced differential returns is an observable phenomenon at least in the credit markets.

Suppose now that tax arbitrage on the part of investors is costly. This changes the slope of the demand curve as discussed in Section 7.3. A rising demand curve generates an equilibrium at the point Y, the point of intersection between the downward sloping supply curve and the upward sloping demand curve. The major effect of introducing costly tax avoidance is to introduce equilibrium differential returns on securities of differential tax status. This is consistent with empirical observation. The implied differential is consistent with a tax rate ranging from zero to the corporate tax rate, τ_c, (assuming that equity returns are not taxed). This implicit rate can no longer be interpreted as the marginal tax rate in any meaningful sense, because, as discussed above, the manner in which the demand curve is generated differs from that of Miller. Thus, this model does not lead to leverage clienteles, contrary to the implication of the Miller equilibrium.

Again, we have an equilibrium quantity of bonds outstanding in the corporate sector, D***, and again, there is an optimal capital structure such that individual firms supply debt until $r^*/(1-\tau_c) - r(D^{***}) = \theta_k(D_k) = \theta(D^{***})$. These implications are identical to the case of costless tax arbitrage, but there are now tax induced differential returns on securities.

7.5 Properties of the Generalized Equilibrium

A significant property of this equilibrium is that interior (optimal) capital structures obtain at the level of individual firms as well as at the aggregate level of the corporate sector. Firms that are able to finance with large amounts of debt before driving marginal agency costs up to the point where they are equal to $r^*/(1-\tau_c) - r(D^{***})$ earn relatively large financial rents. This is because the agency costs on initial units of debt issued are less than $r^*/(1-\tau_c) - r(D^{***})$ and the firm extracts a net tax benefit from issuing them. Firms of this type will conceivably employ higher leverage than will firms for which agency costs rise sharply as additional units of debt are issued.

Several important implications of the equilibrium analysis should be emphasized from the viewpoint of the corporate financial officers. The search for an optimal capital structure may prove to be rewarding. To make an optimal capital structure decision, they must assess (a) the value of the tax savings associated with issuing additional units of debt, and (b) the marginal costs associated with agency problems.

The analysis also has an interesting implication regarding who finally bears the agency costs of debt financing. Jensen and Meckling suggest that rational bondholders will foresee the emergence of agency problems associated with debt financing and will demand compensatory payments in the cost of corporate debt. However, in the equilibrium framework discussed above we find that, once the tax (deduction) benefit of debt financing accrues to debtholders in the form of a "grossed up" interest rate, corporations are enticed to increase their supply of debt only if they are compensated for the associated agency cost disadvantage. Thus, in the same way that the tax subsidy "grosses up" interest rates, agency costs "gross them down." In this *macro* sense, agency costs are borne by bondholders, contrary to the traditional view. Note that, prior to the introduction of the Miller equilibrium, the tax subsidy was viewed as fully accruing to the stockholders of the firm.

Regarding the incidence of the costs of tax arbitrage, we note that these costs increase as tax loopholes are closed, auditing procedures become more efficient, or the costs of intermediation and shortselling rise. Suppose that Congress acts to increase the effective rate of taxation on corporate bond investments by closing some of the existing mechanisms for tax avoidance. Upon first examination, the costs seem to be imposed on individual bond investors, but, as our analysis shows, a new equilibrium will be reached in which interest rates paid on corporate debt will rise. We observe this change through shifts in the location of the demand curve for corporate bonds. The costs of tax arbitrage are the parameters of this curve. If the costs rise, the demand curve moves upward and equilibrium interest rates rise to entice investors to purchase corporate bonds. The elasticity of the demand curve depends on the costs of tax avoidance coupled with the progression and variability of marginal tax rates across investors.

The final incidence of both agency costs and costs of tax arbitrage is determined in a general equilibrium analysis by the elasticities and cross-elasticities of the demand and supply curves of corporate debt. The elasticity of the supply curve depends on the ability of firms to utilize alternative (to interest) tax deductions and on the presence of unresolved agency problems. To the extent that markets are efficient, the fact that the supply curve is less than perfectly elastic may be attributable to the impediments to market resolution of agency problems discussed in Chapter 5. It should be stressed that even if the supply curve is only slightly downward sloping, firms will still reach an interior optimal capital structure by balancing, at the margin, the remaining unresolved agency problems with the "grossed down" interest rate on corporate debt. However, the magnitude of interest rate differential, $r^*(1 - \tau_c) - r(D)$, is small and the impact of changes in capital structure on the value of the firm is slight.

7.6 Conclusion

The introduction of debt related agency costs and a limited form of tax arbitrage by individual investors affect the conclusions associated with the Miller equilibrium. The generalized equilibrium is characterized by the following properties: (1) the corporate capital structure affects market value; (2) the agency costs of debt shared by all firms are shifted to bondholders in the form of lower interest rates; and (3) the observable spread between yields on taxable and nontaxable bonds is explained.

The equilibrium presented in this chapter has important implications to both the financial officer of a publicly traded firm and investors in financial instruments issued by firms. The financial officer should determine the capital structure of the firm according to its specific tax subsidy of debt and agency costs of debt financing. Investors should determine their optimal portfolios based on tax considerations which include the tax exposure of alternative finance instruments and their associated costs of tax arbitrage.[25],[26]

---

[25] The effects of agency problems and costly tax arbitrage exposited in this chapter rely heavily on A. Barnea, R. Haugen, and L. Senbet, "An Equilibrium Analysis of Debt Financing Under Costly Tax Arbitrage and Agency Problems," *Journal of Finance* (June 1981).

[26] In "Portfolio Selection, Capital Structure, and Taxes," Wisconsin Working Paper (April 1984), R. Dammon endogenizes the personal tax structure under an environment in which firms are allowed to issue risky debt. The immediate consequence of this realistic tax schedule is to make marginal personal tax rates *uncertain* or *state-dependent*. Given a standard assumption of fixed investment strategies by firms, Dammon finds an interior capital structure for individual firms, even under corporate supply adjustments à la Miller.

Capital structure irrelevance, on the other hand, requires a more restrictive set of conditions in which firms are allowed to tax arbitrage through simultaneous supply *and* demand adjustments essentially by altering their investment strategies.

```
8888888888888888888888888888888888888888888888888888888888888888888888888888888888888888888
8888888888888888888888888888888888888888888888888888888888888888888888888888888888888888888
88888888888888888888888    8888888888888    888    888    888    8888888888888888888888888
88888888888888888888888888    88888888888    8888    888    888    888888888888888888888888
8888888888888888888888888    888888888    88888    888    888    8888888888888888888888888
88888888888888888888888888    8888888    888888    888    888    888888888888888888888888
8888888888888888888888888888    88888    8888888    888    888    88888888888888888888888
888888888888888888888888888888    888    88888888    888    888    8888888888888888888888
88888888888888888888888888888888    8    888888888    888    888    888888888888888888888
888888888888888888888888888888888    8888888888    888    888    8888888888888888888888
8888888888888888888888888888888888    88888888888    888    888    888888888888888888888
8888888888888888888888888888888888888888888888888888888888888888888888888888888888888888888
8888888888888888888888888888888888888888888888888888888888888888888888888888888888888888888
```

Further Agency Applications

8.1 Introduction

THE foregoing chapters have provided an agency rationale for the existence of complex financial structures and instruments. In this chapter we provide agency applications to other types of contracts and organizational structures, namely investment banking, insurance, financial synergy, and accounting information. The choice of topics seems wide, but it appears that agency theory is sufficiently rich to explain a wide variety of contractual arrangements. It is emphasized that the agency rationale for contracts and organizational structures is not limited to those detailed in this chapter. On the contrary, the purpose of the chapter is to demonstrate the scope and strength of agency theory in rationalizing observable phenomena that are not explained by alternative existing financial theories.

8.2 Insurance and Investment Banking Contracts

8.21 Insurance Contracts[1]

Arrow (1963) provides the basic theorem that, assuming no administrative or information costs, risk averse individuals and risk neu-

---

[1] The subject matter of this section is more fully analyzed in D. Mayers and C. Smith, *Toward a Positive Theory of Insurance*, Monograph Series in Finance and Economics, New York University, 1982 and, by the same authors, "Contractual Provisions, Organizational Structure and Conflict Control in Insurance Markets," *Journal of Business* (July 1981).

tral insurance companies contract for an *optimal* insurance contract with full coverage.[2] However, in reality, we observe a variety of insurance contracts that include deductibles, partial coverage, and upper limits on compensation. Some of these complexities can be explained by the existence of fixed administrative costs per claim.

It can be shown that deductibles, which reduce the number of small claims, also reduce the administrative costs per dollar claimed, leading to a reduction in insurance premiums. Thus, with deductibles a competitive insurance market offers better coverage for a given premium. Still, the administrative cost argument does not explain many other complexities in insurance contracts. For example, it doesn't explain the phenomenon of coinsurance, which is applicable when the insured and insurer share the risk of a policy. Obviously, one may explain coinsurance by optimal risk sharing rules. This requires the assumption that insurance companies behave in accordance with some specified utility function in the same manner as individual investors. However, most insurance companies are publicly held corporations that are presumed to maximize value in a well functioning capital market. It is irrational for value maximizing insurance companies to limit coverage of risk, which is diversifiable by investors who hold their stock as part of a well diversified portfolio. Therefore, risk sharing is a weak argument to explain coinsurance. Another example is the existence of upper limits (maximum coverage) in many insurance contracts (e.g., third party claims in car insurance). Conventional explanations such as risk sharing or administrative costs cannot explain this phenomenon.

Agency theory enriches our understanding of these complexities. Consider the coinsurance phenomenon, which is associated with many health-related insurance programs. Cost sharing provides an economic incentive for the insured to monitor physicians' claims. The insured is best equipped to fulfill the monitoring function, and hence cost sharing may produce an optimal allocation of monitoring costs. Moreover, the relative advantage of the insurance company and the insured in monitoring costs may explain different types of coinsurance and in particular the phenomena of reinsurance when several insurance companies share a particular risk. Consider the upper limit phenomenon. Agency theory provides a rationale for certain classes of insured individuals not to demand insurance against large losses. The rationale is based on limited liability. Large claims on individuals are difficult to collect as the existing bankruptcy laws restrict their en-

---

[2] K. Arrow, "Uncertainty and the Welfare Economics of Medical Care," *American Economic Review* (December 1963).

forcement.[3] The lack of positive incentives to insure oneself against large claims may explain the existence of legal requirements that enforce various types of insurance (e.g., third party car insurance).

8.22 Investment Banking Contracts[4]

Investment banking (underwriting) contracts are associated with the decision of a firm to raise funds through the insurance of stocks or bonds ("going public") in the primary market. The firm approaches an investment banker and delegates the authority to distribute the issue. Several arrangements that differ with respect to their risk sharing aspects are common: (1) a "firm commitment contract" in which the bankers take full responsibility for the distribution of the issue; that is, they absorb all the risks associated with failure to market the issue, (2) a "best effort" contract in which the issuer bears all the risk, and (3) a "standby contract" in which the risk is shared. As explained in Section 6.2, each of these contracts may be first-best, depending on the risk attitudes of each of the contracting parties. For example, if the issuer is risk neutral, the "best effort" contract is optimal. These first-best contracts collapse when the distribution effort invested by the banker is unobservable after the fact. The contract must be specified so as to provide an incentive for the banker to invest the level of efforts that the issuer prefers. In general, the banker will prefer to take actions that are not necessarily in the best interest of the issuer.[5] The type of second-best contracts that arise depend on the ability of the issuer to monitor the banker's efforts. For the case of *unobservable* efforts, a contract that includes a bonus paid to the banker if the issue is sold out may be optimal, as it encourages the banker to expand efforts to complete the distribution of the issue.

The investment banking case is interesting because it illuminates

---

[3] Note the similarity between this argument and the analysis for stockholders' incentives to bear unwarranted risk (Section 3.32). The existence of insurance commitments in bond covenants is well understood within the framework of agency theory, as insurance serves to monitor the level of risk to which the firm is exposed.

[4] The structuring of optimal investment banking contracts was considered by G. Mandelker and A. Raviv, "Investment Banking: An Economic Analysis of Optimal Underwriting Contracts," *Journal of Finance* (June 1977) and by D. Baron and B. Holmstrom "The Incentive Problem and the Design of Investment Banking Contracts for New Issues Under Asymmetric Information," *Journal of Finance* (December 1980).

[5] The banker's decisions are related to the price of the issue and to the level of efforts. The higher the issue price, the more distribution efforts are required to market the issue. The combination of price and efforts, given a prespecified commission schedule, may not coincide with the interests of the issuer.

several issues that were discussed in previous chapters (see Sections 3.2 and 6.2):

1. The ability of agency theory to explain complex contracts
2. The extent to which agency problems are resolved if perfect monitoring of efforts is available
3. The ability of well functioning markets to at least partially resolve agency problems—in this case, if the market for underwriting services is informationally efficient, the banker may have to face an implicit penalty in the form of loss of future business if he fails to deliver.

8.3 Agency Problems and Financial Synergy

Synergy occurs when two or more firms or ventures are united, and the whole is worth more (or less) than the sum of its parts. For our own purposes, we can categorize synergy into two parts, economic and financial. *Economic synergy* stems from the effect of merger on the manner in which the firm conducts its operations, or its effect on the competitive environment in which the firm purchases its factors of production or sells its products. Horizontal mergers may reduce the level of competition or increase operating efficiency through economies of scale. Either may make the value of the merged firm greater than the sum of its composite parts. Vertical mergers may be synergistic if they make possible greater efficiency in the acquisition of supplies and materials or in the assembly and distribution of the product. As its name would imply, *financial synergy* occurs when a merger is accompanied by an increase (or reduction) in the total wealth of all securityholders in the combined firm, or by a transfer of wealth between securityholders (for example, bondholders and stockholders), that can be related to the manner in which the firm is financed. In other words, economic synergy is related to the composition and management of the assets on the left-hand side of the balance sheet, while financial synergy is related to the composition of the claims to the assets on the right-hand side of the balance sheet.

One form of financial synergy that occurs in merger is called the coinsurance effect. Consider a single period analysis under risk neutrality and two firms that are not perfectly correlated, but have identical probability distributions for the ending value of their assets. Both firms have debt outstanding with a fixed claim to the ending value of the firm equal to D. There is some probability that the ending value of either firm will be less than the bondholders' claim, in which case the bondholders will receive less than the full value of their promised claim. The market values of the bonds of both firms reflect these probabilities and are priced at V_D. The value of the common stock for each firm is given by $V_S = V - V_D$, where V is the total market value of the assets of each firm. Suppose the firms now merge. The bondholders' claim to the ending assets of the merged firm is now 2D. However, since the firms are less than perfectly correlated, the variance of the distribution of the ending value of the combined firm is less than twice that of the firms as individuals entities. As a consequence, the probability of default is now less than before the merger. As a result, the total market value of the debt of the merged firm is now greater than $2V_D$. Since, by assumption, there are no *economic* forms of synergy, the total value of the assets of the merged firm is 2V. As a consequence, the total value of the common stock is less than $2V_S$. The merger fails to create new wealth, but it does result in a *transfer* of wealth from stockholders to bondholders, and the transfer can be related to the fixed nature of the bondholders' claim. Alternatively, the combined firm can issue more debt and still preserve the (per unit) premerger values of debt. In this sense financial synergy increases the (optimal) debt capacity.

In Section 8.31 below we consider a form of financial synergy that is related to a particular agency problem, the risk incentive problem. As we shall see, agency-related synergy is unique in that, in addition to producing wealth transfers such as the one associated with coinsurance, it may induce changes in the composition and management of the firm's assets that are related to the composition of the firm's capital structure. Thus, it may make the aggregate value of the combined firm worth more than the sum of its parts.

8.31 Synergy Induced by the Risk Incentive Problem

Figure 8.1 is similar in form to Figure 4.6. Assume we are dealing with a firm that has a single investment opportunity. Management has some degree of flexibility in managing the venture. By altering the production function they can produce changes in both the risk σ and the market value of the venture. The circle in Figure 8.1 represents the boundary in which they can alter the risk and market value of the investment opportunity. Management can, at its discretion, take a position anywhere within the interior or on the parameter of the circle. For convenience, in later discussion we have scaled the value of the investment V_1 by its required capital commitment, I.

As explained in previous chapters, if the firm were to finance the investment entirely with equity capital, it would adopt the value maximizing strategy at point E. Suppose instead it finances the investment in part by issuing a debt security with a fixed claim equal to D. In this case we can once again consider the stock as if it were an option to acquire the entire firm from the bondholders at an exercise price equal to D. The value of this option increases with increases in both the market value and the variance of the underlying asset, or, in this case, the investment opportunity. Each of the broken curves $V_{S3/I}$, $V_{S2/I}$, and $V_{S1/I}$ represents a locus of points representing a given market value for the common stock. It is the case that $V_{S1} > V_{S2} >$

Figure 8.1. Synergy Associated with the Risk Incentive Problem

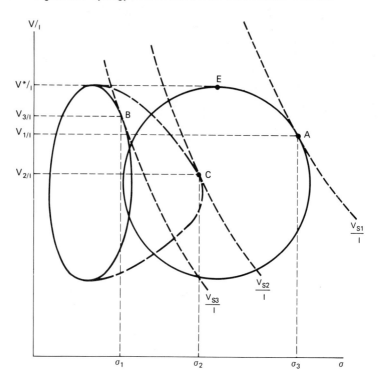

V_{S3}. Thus, stock values increase as one moves to the northeast on the diagram, with increasing values for both the variance and the value of the underlying asset. Given management's objective to maximize the value of common stock, they attempt to be on the highest iso-curve for stock valuation. The strategy consistent with this objective is located at the point of tangency, A, with the investment opportunity set. This, of course, falls short of the total asset value maximizing strategy by an amount, $V^* - V_1$. As explained in previous chapters, rational bondholders will anticipate this in their offering price for the debt, and the agency cost, $V^* - V_1$, is borne by the firm's stockholders.

As more debt is issued by increasing the bondholder's claim, D, the negative slopes of the broken curves become more pronounced, and the point of tangency slips further down the circle increasing the magnitude of the agency cost. The associated marginal agency cost function for the firm is depicted in Figure 8.2 as MC_1.

Suppose we have a modified bond market equilibrium, as described in Chapter 7, in which a downward sloping supply curve for debt produces a tax-induced premium in the interest rate on bonds that serves to *partially* offset their tax advantage to the firm. A partial tax advantage remains and when expressed as a percent of the market value of the debt, it is equal to OA in Figure 8.2. Given this, it is in the interest of the firm to issue debt until its marginal agency cost is equal to its marginal tax advantage at point B. Since, for all previous units of debt issued, the marginal agency cost is less than the marginal tax advantage, the firm earns a financier's surplus equal to the area in rectangle ABCD. The surplus is determined by the excess of the marginal tax saving over the average cost of agency, A_{C1}, and the associated level of debt financing.

Now, introduce a second firm into the analysis. Assume it also has a single investment opportunity, and by changing the production function, it can alter the risk and market value of the project in identical fashion to the first firm. Thus, for simplicity only, we assume that the circle of Figure 8.1 represents the *shape* of the investment opportunity set for both firms. The investment opportunities themselves are not identical, in the sense that the returns from these investments need not be perfectly correlated. Moreover, the degree to which they are correlated may depend on the selection of individual strategies by each firm from within their respective investment opportunity sets.

Given our assumptions, the second firm faces the same marginal agency cost function as the first firm, and it issues the same amount of debt and captures the same financier's surplus. Suppose, however, that the two firms merge. We now have a single firm with two non-mutually exclusive projects, the strategy for each of which is selected from the circle(s) of Figure 8.1. The united firm can be considered as a portfolio of the two projects.

Figure 8.2. Marginal and Average Agency Cost Functions

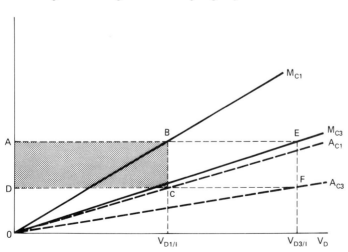

Consider the market value and standard deviation properties of the portfolio of the assets of the combined firms. While we can simply add the market values of selected strategies to obtain the market value of the portfolio, we cannot simply add, or to be more precise, average the standard deviations. Because the projects are not perfectly correlated, the standard deviation of the portfolio is less than an average of the standard deviation of its parts. Thus, while the opportunity set for each project is represented by the circle, the opportunity set for the portfolio of projects is represented by the shaded oval of Figure 8.1.

Note that it is now in the interest of the merged firm to adopt the combined strategy represented by point B in the diagram.[6] Consider first that the agency cost is reduced to $V^* - V_3$. Moreover, the market value of the debt that can be raised while incurring this cost is greater than before. This is true because (a) the total market value of the combined firm as a percent of the required investment is now greater and (b) the total market value of the common stock as a percent of I is now smaller ($V_{S1} > V_{S3}$). As a result, for any given total of debt issued, the marginal agency cost incurred by the combined firm is less than the sum of the marginal agency costs incurred by the two firms as individual entities. Thus, the merger results in a shift in the marginal agency cost function, such as from MC_1 to MC_3 in Figure 8.2. As a result, we have an increase in the relative amount of debt issued, and an increase in the financier's surplus to AEFD. The whole is worth more than the sum of its parts.

This result, of course, is specific to the nature of the assumed opportunity sets of Figure 8.1. Suppose that the returns for the lower valued strategies for the firms happened to be more highly correlated with one another. This would imply a lower reduction in risk when these strategies are combined than when the higher valued strategies are combined. In this case, the opportunity set for the merged firm might take a more triangular shape, and bring us to a stock value maximizing strategy at point C. At this point, the agency cost is greater and the associated market value of the debt issued may well be lower than at point A. Here a merger results in a shift upward in the marginal agency cost function and a reduction in the financier's surplus. Agency costs now act as a disincentive to merger, or if the two firms are already united it provides an incentive for them to "spin off" from one another.

_____

[6] We have assumed that for the merged firm, the bondholder's claim, as a fraction of the total required investment, is equal to that of the debt issued by both the individual firms.

8.32 Synergy Induced by the Other Agency Problems

In general, the marginal agency cost function reflects a composite of all the agency problems faced by the firm. To the extent that merger has an impact on these problems, financial synergy may arise from a number of sources. Consider the agency cost associated with bankruptcy; merger may affect the cost associated with bankruptcy in at least two ways. First, there may exist economies of scale in resolving disputes between bondholders and stockholders. If so, the *direct* costs of bankruptcy may be smaller for the larger firm, at least when expressed as a percentage of the total value of the bankrupt firm. It is less likely that there are economies of scale associated with the indirect costs of bankruptcy (such as disruption in the relationships with suppliers or customers), however. In any case, merger may result in a reduction in the overall percentage of the firm consumed by the bankruptcy proceedings. Second, to the extent that the returns associated with two merging firms are less than perfectly correlated, merger may reduce the probability of the total return falling below the total value of the bondholders' claims. If this is true, even if merger has no impact on the actual magnitude of bankruptcy costs, it does have an impact on their expected value. In any case, it is likely that the agency cost associated with bankruptcy induces a synergistic property that acts to promote merger.

Synergy may also originate from the investment incentive problem. Recall that this problem stems from the incentive that debt financing provides to forgo otherwise profitable investment opportunities. Returning to Figure 4.7, remember that the firm makes the investment at the end of period 1 in all states to the right of S_a. That is, the investment is made in all states where the market value of the option to make the investment exceeds the required capital commitment, I. In the presence of debt that matures at the end of period 2 with promised payment D, the investment is made only in states lying to the right of S_b. The cost to the firm is represented by the shaded area AGB. Doubling the promised payment increases the cost to AFC. Here the shape of the marginal agency cost function can be related to the shape of the function AGFE. It is depicted here to be linear, but of course it need not be.

The synergistic properties of this agency problem derive from the fact that if we unite two firms, each with a particular value-state profile, the value-state profile of the united firm again may bear little relationship to the profiles of its constituent parts. To see this, recognize that the ordering of the states is unique to each of the individual firms and to the merged firm. The states are merely ordered on the basis of the associated market values of the investment option. Since the value-state profile of the merged firm (partially) determines its marginal agency cost function, the financier's surplus of the merged firm is likely to be more (or less) than the sum of its constituent parts. Thus, the investment incentive problem may provide an incentive promoting either mergers or spin-offs.

8.4 Agency Problems and Accounting Information

The role of accounting information in agency models can be examined in two complementary ways. First, we examine the ability of accounting information to resolve agency problems. In a two-person agency model (Section 3.2), accounting information plays a major role in structuring enforceable managerial contracts. In financial models (Section 3.3), accounting information is utilized in complex contractual arrangements (e.g., bond covenants) between bondholders and stockholders. Second, we utilize elements of agency theory to better understand the emergence and structure of accounting information itself. The lack of a theoretical framework in accounting analysis has been noticed by many financial writers. Rigorous positive theory that explains and predicts particular accounting procedures and disclosures is not yet available. Agency theory may provide a building block for such a theory; by so doing, it will enhance the development of the field.

This section focuses on the role of accounting information in agency models, with particular emphasis on the properties of accounting numbers that make them suitable for resolution of agency problems. First, we consider managerial accounting procedures (budgets, variance investigations), which are analyzed in the context of a two person agency model. It is shown that particular managerial accounting procedures are useful in structuring contractual relationships between agents (managers) and principals (owners). Next, we consider financial accounting information that is reported to external users under the guidelines of General Accepted Accounting Principles (GAAP) and auditors' verification. This information is useful for the (partial) resolution of agency problems in financial models.

8.41 The Role of Accounting Information in the Two-Person Agency Model

The analysis of a two-person agency model in Sections 3.2 and 6.2 focuses on the importance of information relating to the motivation of agents and to the efficient distribution of risk. Perfect information (i.e., information that allows *ex post* measurement of the agent choices) leads to the structuring of first-best employment and compensation contracts for managers. Imperfect information (e.g., information that doesn't allow the measurement of agents' contribution net of the effect of uncontrollable events) leads to the loss of welfare generated either by inefficient allocation of risk and/or suboptimal behavior by agents.

The demand for accounting information is studied in the context of the informational requirements of agency models. Accounting information is useful if (a) it provides information relating to the measurement of agents' performance and decision choices[7] and (b) if it can be independently and unambiguously observed by both the principal and the agent. Thus, agency theory is capable of explaining and justifying the generation of accounting information. Hence, the scope of accounting information, together with other sources of information, dictates the type and complexity of contracts between principal and agents.

In most cases, full information, i.e., information on agents' actions, is not costlessly available. Limited information produces second-best contracts. Improvement in contracts is always weighted against the costs involved in getting more and better information. Hence, the set of enforceable contracts depends on the costs and availability of information that can effectively monitor the agents' choices and ability. In this context, it is appropriate to evaluate the accuracy of accounting measures of managerial performance. Obviously, if these measures lack accuracy, or if their preparation is costly, agency problems are not completely resolved.

Recent literature in accounting theory examines the role of particular accounting procedures in resolving agency problems. The emphasis is on managerial accounting systems.[8] Important works in this area are the studies by Demski (1976) and Demski and Feltham (1978). The consistency of managerial accounting principles and techniques with the information requirements of agency models is offered as a foundation for a comprehensive theory of accounting.

Managerial accounting measures of performance are based on the concept of "responsibility," measuring the extent to which management is successful in utilizing those corporate resources over which it has full control. Measurement of performance based on the responsibility criterion is consistent with the agency model if the "states of the world" are known with certainty. In this case, performance is directly attributable to the manager (agent) effort and a first-best contract based on performance is feasible. But under uncertainty, and

---

[7] As explained in Section 3.2, managerial performance is assessed in a broad sense. Thus, perfect, after-the-fact information must indicate managerial choice of actions (e.g., which of a set of possible projects was selected), decision on the level of efforts, managerial choice on "perk" consumption, etc. To facilitate first-best contractual arrangements between management and owners, such information must be independent of the effect of uncontrollable events ("states of nature").

[8] This section draws heavily from "Agency Research in Managerial Accounting: A Survey," by S. Baiman, Working Paper, University of Pittsburgh. The implications of agency theory research to financial accounting are analyzed in A. Atkinson and G. Feltham, "Agency Theory Research and Financial Accounting Standards," Working Paper, University of British Columbia (1981).

when the information is not sufficient to infer managerial performance net of the effect of uncontrollable events, responsibility accounting may not be consistent with the informational requirements of the
agency model. Relevant information on management choices may also
require information on the performance of *other* managers; with this
information, one can sort out the uncontrollable state of the world
and, consequently, provide a better estimate of the choices made by
managers.

The literature also considers the conditions under which budgets
and variance investigation policies satisfy the informational requirements of an agency model. The budget is basically a norm that allows
the definition of a favorable outcome ("above the budget") and an
unfavorable outcome ("below the budget"). Structuring compensation
schemes based on budgets improves the monitoring of agents in specified scenarios.

One of the more interesting features in this analysis is the theoretical
justification for *ex post* monitoring. Economists have often raised questions regarding the optimality of *ex post* investigation when the inves-
tigated costs are "sunk." Similar questions are raised regarding the
optimality of arbitrary cost allocations, including the allocation of
fixed overhead costs. Agency theory provides a reasonable rationale
for such procedures by demonstrating the effect of allocations on
motivation and by offering a link between an agent's choice of action
(in an *ex ante* sense) and the forthcoming investigation.[9]

8.42 An Illustration

To see the effect of imperfect measurement of managerial performance, consider the case where the performance of a financial
manager is assessed by net earnings. Suppose also that managerial
compensation is based on the difference between the percentage change
in earnings and the percentage change in earnings of a median firm
within the industry. The median firm serves as a flexible norm, which
mitigates the effects of uncontrollable events on performance measurement. The distortionary effects of such compensation schemes can
be verified by analyzing the decision choices of an agent among various investments that produce different levels of risk and return.

The agent will search for investments producing high current earnings without regard to their value. Obviously, if the firm is publicly
traded, linking compensation to the market value of its securities will
mitigate some of the agency problems. Suppose, however, that the
manager heads a division or heads a nonpublic firm. Reliance on
earnings to measure performance may distort decision making, as the
following example clearly shows.

---

[9] The optimality of cost allocation is studied in J. Zimmerman, "The Costs and Benefits
of Cost Allocation," *The Accounting Review* (July 1979).

A manager of a company has to decide on the terms of a long-term loan to be given to a third party. The loan is for ten years, paying a floating interest rate of prime plus 2 percent. The cost of funds to the company is prime plus 1 percent. The borrower agrees to an alternative agreement by which the loan will carry interest of prime plus 1 percent and an additional 5 percent up-front commission. From the point of view of the credit granting company this alternative is obviously inferior. The commission does not cover the present value of 1 percent per year and it may also require additional taxes. But note that earnings would be increased. The manager may well choose the second alternative, thereby reducing corporate wealth but improving his performance. The example thus suggests a considerable agency cost due to imperfect monitoring of managers' performance.

This illustration is only one example of the distortionary effects of imperfect performance information on managerial decision making. Recent literature in accounting attempts to assess managerial choices among different reporting procedures that affect reported earnings and corporate taxes. Inventory valuation is an important example. Corporations are allowed to choose between LIFO and FIFO methods to value inventories. Under inflation, the LIFO method reduces the value of inventories (which is based on early purchases) and reduces current reported earnings and taxes. However, a shift to LIFO may also affect management compensation if it is linked to reported earnings.[10]

Several studies analyze the role of managerial compensation packages in determining choices among different reporting methods. The results are conflicting but at least some studies report a significant effect of the compensation plan on management choices.[11]

The analysis has thus far considered the choice among reporting alternatives by the management of a firm. The formation of these alternatives is done by professional standard setting boards such as the Financial Accounting Standards Board (FASB). The board considers the views of both management and public accountants before any new standard or a change in existing standards becomes the rule. Several interesting studies on the choice of positions by management

---

[10] A detailed anlaysis of the decision to change to LIFO appears in A. Rashad Abdel-Khalik, "The Decision to Change to LIFO: The Role of Executive Compensation and the Political Cost Hypothesis," Working Paper, University of Illinois at Urbana-Champaign (June 1983). The empirical evidence that is provided in this study suggests that executive compensation is not a motivating factor in the choice of LIFO.

[11] In these studies, the existence of earnings-based compensation plans for management is represented by a 0–1 dummy variable. The significance of this variable in explaining the choice of an income-increasing reporting alternative is considered a test for the existence of agency costs. A detailed analysis of this procedure appears in Hagerman and Zmijenski, "Some Economic Determinants of Accounting Policy Choice," *Journal of Accounting and Economics* (August 1979) and by the same authors, "An Income Strategy Approach to the Positive Theory of Accounting Standards Setting/Choice," *Journal of Accounting and Economics* (August 1981).

and certified public accountants provide convincing evidence that self-interest, or wealth-maximizing considerations, play a major role in determining the position taken by particular managers or auditors.[12]

Political considerations, i.e., decisions made in order to satisfy perceived regulations on potential antitrust actions, play a major role in determining managerial choices among alternative reporting procedures. An agent (management) is faced with a potential threat to corporate (and personal) wealth stemming from government actions and regulations, which may be triggered by reports on corporate performance. Several studies attempt to quantify the effect of (potential) government intervention on managerial choices, particularly with respect to reporting alternatives.[13] While the results are still preliminary, they indicate that the agency framework is sufficiently rich in explaining management decision making in areas where no alternative explanation existed.

8.43 The Role of Accounting Information in Financial Contracts

The production and public disclosure of accounting information can potentially reduce the costs associated with agency problems in financial contracts. Two properties of accounting numbers are considered in this regard: (a) their objectivity,[14] and (b) their detail. The *objectivity* property is required to overcome the problem of moral hazard, since numbers (signals) that are produced (manipulated) by management cannot serve as unambiguous measures of performance. *Detailed* information is required for an effective *ex post* monitoring of management performance.

The availability of objective and detailed data on corporate performance is a necessary condition for the construction of certain complex contractual arrangements between classes of securityholders (e.g., bond covenants). Complex contracts (e.g., bond contracts that include covenants restricting risk taking on the part of management) contribute to the resolution of conflicts of interest that may exist between these parties. The previous section analyzed the issue of managerial compensation which is frequently conditioned upon the realized values of certain accounting numbers. This represents an attempt to evaluate the performance of the mergers net of the effect of uncontrollable events. The purpose of this incentive arrangement is to align

---

[12] See R. Watts and J. Zimmerman, "Towards a Positive Theory of the Determination of Accounting Standards," *The Accounting Review* (January 1978).

[13] Abdel-Khalik, *op. cit.*, provides a summary of these studies.

[14] This property implies that accounting information is based on factual data. That is, the original transaction values used for accounting measurement and valuation are more verifiable than measurement and valuation under alternative models. The auditor's role in the verification of disclosed information is particularly important in this regard.

the interests of management with the interests of the firm's security-holders.

Bond covenants are designed to impose limits on managements' (stockholders') freedom to choose among the alternative investment and financing packages that determine the level of risk of the firms' assets. Such covenants protect the bondholders in serving as a disincentive for management to engage in high-risk activities on behalf of stockholders.[15] Also, if accounting numbers are produced in sufficient detail they allow for more accurate measurement of risk so that bond covenants can be set to more effectively control risk in an *ex ante* sense. Thus, the agency problems associated with the risk incentive in debt financing are mitigated. One example that demonstrates this property of detailed data is the requirement to report performance by lines of business. Data on divisional performance can be used in bond covenants restricting management to operate to pre-specified degrees in lines of business that are less risky than others.

We stress, however, that bond covenants based on accounting numbers cannot resolve the risk incentive problem completely. Statistics from financial statements (e.g., financial ratios) that are used in bond covenants to control the level of risk have severe measurement limitations. Also, while mitigating the agency problems of risk incentives, bond covenants may create new problems as the firm, faced with constraints on its opportunity set, may be forced to forgo profitable (but high-risk) projects and suboptimize financial policies (e.g., the dividend constraint).[16,17]

Public disclosure of accounting data may serve to mitigate agency problems associated with informational asymmetry. That is, accounting numbers may contribute to the ability of the market to distinguish the firm from other, less profitable firms. The usefulness of accounting numbers to forecast the relevant parameters of the return distri-

---

[15] See C. Smith and J. Warner, "On Financial Contracting: An Analysis of Bond Covenants," *Journal of Financial Economics* (June 1979) for an analysis of the role of bond covenants and A. Barnea, R. Haugen and L. Senbet, "Market Imperfections, Agency Problems, and Capital Structure: A Review," *Financial Management* (Summer 1981) for an analysis of the role of complex securities in mitigating agency problems.

[16] The effect of dividend constraints on the choice of investments is discussed in K. John and A. Kalay, "Stockholder-Bondholder Conflict and Dividend Constraints," *Journal of Financial Economics*, (July 1982).

[17] Accounting numbers may also serve to mitigate the problem of forgone investment opportunities in order to expropriate bondholder wealth. The flow-of-funds statement might be expanded to include details relating the capital expenditures for the previous accounting period. These numbers enable a monitoring of the existing allocation of capital within the firm. Information relating to the profitability of alternative investment projects (even those not undertaken by the firm) may be inferred from the accounting reports of other firms. Thus, accounting information may be useful not only in assessing the profitability of projects that were undertaken by the firm, but also the profitability of projects in the firm's opportunity set.

bution has been evaluated in many empirical studies.[18] It is apparent that audited accounting reports are useful in predicting future returns and that at least some level of disaggregation produces information that contributes to the quality of forecasts of corporate performance.

Public disclosure may also increase the effectiveness of capital and labor markets in disciplining management to make decisions that maximize total firm value. This is so because detailed, objective, and publicly disclosed numbers may assist firms in making assessments of the relative performance of managements of other firms. The numbers may serve to reduce the asymmetry of information between the manager, the firm, and other firms. Accounting numbers may also enable potential *acquirers* to assess whether existing management makes value-maximizing production and financial decisions and thus may facilitate the process of arbitrage through takeover.

On the other hand, a wide range of accounting procedures for external users is still in discretionary use by management for producing income figures. For instance, accounting methods for depreciation, inventory valuation, consolidation, investment tax credit, etc., vary so widely that firms with similar economic characteristics may end up establishing very different accounting numbers. These variations limit the scope of accounting in resolving agency problems and, therefore, one would *a priori* expect attempts to minimize these variations and to achieve objectivity and consistency not only vertically but horizontally across different firms. Horizontal uniformity facilitates comparison of performance, and hence it promotes the role of accounting in resolving agency problems. However, in view of the potential ability of accounting numbers to reduce agency problems, it is surprising that management and stockholders are not more uniformly supportive of additional disclosure requirements, as well as attempts to standardize accounting.[19]

---

[18] See G. Foster, *Financial Statement Analysis* (Englewood Cliffs, N.J.: Prentice-Hall, June 1978) (ch. 9) for a review of this literature. Of particular interest are studies that evaluate the performance of predictions of systematic risk and expected return using accounting data compared to predictions based on naïve models e.g., W. Beaver, P. Kettler and M. Scholes, "The Association Between Market Determined and Accounting Determined Risk Measures," *Accounting Review* (October 1970), B. Rosenberg and V. Marathe, "The Prediction of Investment Risk: Systematic and Residual Risk," Reprint 21, Berkeley Working Paper Series.

[19] An explanation of this attitude is offered in Section 7.4. It is shown that in bond market equilibrium (at least some of) the agency costs of debt are borne by bondholders. This reduces the incentive of stockholders or management to engage in improvements in the scope and detail of accounting disclosures because the resulting benefits may be directed to bondholders.

8.5 Conclusion

Further agency applications have been demonstrated by using examples for the insurance and investment banking areas. The chapter also contains an analysis of the role of accounting information in agency models. The analysis leads to new insights on the structure and properties of accounting information. On one hand, agency theory provides a foundation for the construction of a positive theory of accounting. On the other hand, the structure of complex contracts is better understood by the limitations of the accounting information on which they are based. The effect of financial merger on corporate wealth and the distribution of this wealth among a firm's claimholders is analyzed in Section 8.3. Again, agency theory enriches this discussion by providing new insights not available from competing theories of financial mergers.

References

Abdel-Khalik, A., "The Decision to Change to LIFO: The Role of Executive Compensation and the Political Cost Hypothesis," University of Illinois Working Paper (June 1983).

Akerlof, G., "The Market for Lemons: Quality Uncertainty and the Market Mechanism," *Quarterly Journal of Economics* 85 (August 1970).

Alchian, A. A. and H. Demsetz, "Production, Information Costs, and Economic Organization," *American Economic Review* (December 1972).

Amershi, A., "Agency Theory: Clarifications, Consolidation and Extensions," Unpublished Working Paper, Stanford University (1980).

Amihud, Y. and B. Lev, "Risk Reduction as a Managerial Motive for Conglomerate Mergers," *Bell Journal of Economics* (Autumn 1981).

Arrow, K., "Optimal Insurance and Generalized Deductibles," R-1108-0E0, The Rand Corporation (February 1973).

Arrow, K. and G. Debreu, "Existence of an Equilibrium for a Competitive Economy," *Econometrica* 22 (1954).

Atkinson, A. and G. A. Feltham, "Information in Capital Markets: An Agency Theory Perspective," Unpublished Working Paper, Faculty of Commerce, University of British Columbia (January 1981).

Atkinson, A. A., "Information Incentives in a Standard-Setting Model of Control," *Journal of Accounting Research* (Spring 1979).

146

Auerbach, A., "Taxation, Corporate Financial Policy and the Cost of Capital," *Journal of Economic Literature* (September 1983).

Auman, R., "Agreeing to Disagree," *Annals of Statistics* 4 (1980).

Aivazian, V. and J. Callen, "Corporate Leverage and Growth: The Game Theoretic Issues," *Journal of Financial Economics* (December 1980).

Azariadis, C., "Implicit Contracts and Related Topics: A Survey," Unpublished Working Paper, University of Pennsylvania (November 1980).

Bailey, Jr., A. and W. J. Boe, "Goal and Resource Transfers in the Multigoal Organization," *Accounting Review* (July 1976).

Baiman, S. and J. S. Demski, "Variance Analysis Procedures as Motivation Devices," *Management Science* (August 1980a).

Baiman, S., "The Evaluation and Choice of Internal Information Systems Within a Multi-person World," *Journal of Accounting Research* (Spring 1971).

Barnea, A., R. Haugen, and L. Senbet, "Market Imperfections, Agency Problems, and Capital Structure: A Review," *Financial Management* (September 1981).

Barnea, A., R. Haugen, and L. Senbet, "An Equilibrium Analysis of Debt Financing Under Costly Tax Arbitrage and Agency Problems," *Journal of Finance* (June 1981).

Barnea, A., R. Haugen, and L. Senbet, "A Rationale for Debt Maturity Structure and Call Provisions in the Agency Theoretic Framework," *Journal of Finance* (December 1980).

Baron, D. and B. Holmstrom, "The Investment Banking Contract for New Issues under Asymmetric Information: Delegation and the Incentives Problem," *Journal of Finance* (December 1980).

Baron, D., "Default Risk, Homemade Leverage, and the Modigliani-Miller Theorem," *American Economic Review* (March 1974).

Baxter, N., "Leverage, Risk of Ruin and the Cost of Capital," *Journal of Finance* (September 1967).

Bhattacharya, S., "Nondissipative Signaling Structures and Dividend Policy," *Quarterly Journal of Economics* 95 (August 1980).

Bhattacharya, S., "Imperfect Information, Dividend Policy, and the 'Bird in the Hand' Fallacy," *Bell Journal of Economics* (Spring 1979).

Black, F. and M. Scholes, "The Pricing of Options and Corporate Liabilities," *Journal of Political Economy* (May–June 1973).

Bodie, Z. and R. Taggart, "Future Investment Opportunities and the Value of the Call Provision on a Bond," *Journal of Finance* (September 1978).

Borch, K., "Equilibrium in a Reinsurance Market," *Econometrica* 3 (1962).

Boyce, W. and A. Kalotay, "Tax Differentials and Callable Bonds," *Journal of Finance* (September 1979).

Brennan, M., "Taxes, Market Valuation and Corporation Financial Policy," *National Tax Journal* (December 1970).

Brennan, M. and E. Schwartz, "Corporate Income Taxes, Valuation and the Problem of Optimal Capital Structure," *Journal of Business* (January 1978).

Buser, S., A. Chen, and E. Kane, "Federal Deposit Insurance, Regulatory Policy, and Optimal Bank Capital," *Journal of Finance* (March 1981).

Campbell, T. and W. Kracaw, "Information Production, Market Signalling, and the Theory of Financial Intermediation," *Journal of Finance* (September 1980).

Christensen, J., "Communication and Coordination in Agencies: An Approach to Participative Budgeting," Unpublished Working Paper, Stanford University (May 1979).

Cornell, B. and R. Roll, "Strategies for Pairwise Competitions in Markets and Organizations," *Bell Journal of Economics* (Spring 1981).

Dammon, R., "A Theory of Corporate Financial Policy Under Progressive Personal Taxation," Ph.D. Thesis, University of Wisconsin–Madison (August 1984).

DeAngelo, H. and R. Masulis, "Optimal Capital Structure Under Corporate and Personal Taxation," *Journal of Financial Economics* (March 1980).

Demski, J. S. and G. Feltham, "Economic Incentives and Budgetary Control Systems," *Accounting Review* (April 1978).

Demski, J. and G. Feltham, *Cost Determination: A Conceptual Approach*, Ames, IA: Iowa State University Press (1977).

Diamond, D. and R. Verrechia, "Optimal Managerial Contracts and Equilibrium Security Prices," *Journal of Finance* (May 1982).

Dittman, D. and P. Prakash, "Cost Variance Investigation: Markovian Control Versus Optimal Control," *Accounting Review* (April 1979).

Dopuch, N. J., G. Birnberg and J. S. Demski, "An Extension of a Standard Cost Variance Analysis," *Accounting Review* (July 1967).

Dothan, U. and J. Williams, "Debt, Investment Opportunities and Agency," Northwestern University Working Paper (1981).

Dyckman, T., "The Investigation of Cost Variances," *Journal of Accounting Research* (Autumn 1969).

Dye, R. A., "Optimal Contract Length," Unpublished Working Paper, Carnegie-Mellon University (April 1980).

Elton, E. and M. Gruber, "The Economic Value of the Call Option," *Journal of Finance* (September 1972).

Evans, J. H. III, "Optimal Contracts with Costly Conditional Auditing," Supplement to *Journal of Accounting Research* (1980).

Fama, E. F., "Agency Problems and the Theory of the Firm," *Journal of Political Economy* (April 1980).

Fama, E., "The Effects of a Firm's Investment and Financing Decisions on the Welfare of Its Security Holders," *American Economic Review* 68 (June 1978).

Fama, E. and M. Jensen, "Agency Problems and Residual Claims," *Journal of Law and Economics* (June 1983).

Feltham, G., "The Value of Information," *The Accounting Review* (October 1968).

Foster, G., *Financial Statement Analysis* (Englewood Cliffs, NJ: Prentice-Hall, 1978).

Galai, D. and R. Masulis, "The Option Pricing Model and the Risk Factor of Stock," *Journal of Financial Economics* (January–March 1976).

Green, R., "Investment Incentives, Debt, and Warrants," *Journal of Financial Economics* (March 1984).

Gjesdal, F., "Accounting for Stewardship," *Journal of Accounting Research* (Spring 1981).

Grossman, S. and J. Stiglitz, "On Value Maximization and Alternative Objectives of the Firm," *Journal of Finance* (May 1977).

Grossman, J. and J. Stiglitz, "Information and Competitive Price Systems," *American Economic Review* (May 1976).

Groves, T. and M. Loeb, "Incentives in Divisionalized Firms," *Management Science* (March 1979).

Groves, T. and J. O. Ledyard, "Optimal Allocation of Public Goods: A Solution to the 'Free Rider' Problem," *Econometrica* (May 1977).

Hagen, K., "Default Risk, Homemade Leverage, and the Modigliani-Miller Theorem: A Note," *American Economic Review* (March 1976).

Hagerman, R. and Zmijenski, "Some Economic Determinants of Accounting Policy Choice," *Journal of Accounting and Economics* (August 1979).

Hakansson, N., "Interim Disclosure and Public Forecasts: An Economic Analysis and a Framework for Choice," *Accounting Review* (April 1977).

Harris, M. and R. M. Townsend, "Resource Allocation Under Asymmetric Information," *Econometrica* (January 1981).

Harris, M. and A. Raviv, "Optimal Incentive Contracts with Imperfect Information," *Journal of Economic Theory* (December 1979).

Harris, M. and A. Raviv, "Some Results on Incentive Contracts," *American Economic Review* (March 1978).

Hayes, D. C., "The Contingency Theory of Managerial Accounting," *Accounting Review* (January 1977).

Haugen, R. and L. Senbet, "Resolving the Agency Problems of External Capital through Stock Options," *Journal of Finance* (June 1981).

Haugen, R. and L. Senbet, "New Perspectives on Informational Asymmetry and Agency Relationships," *Journal of Financial and Quantitative Analysis* (November 1979).

Haugen, R. and L. Senbet, "The Insignificance of Bankruptcy Costs to the Theory of Optimal Capital Structure," *Journal of Finance* (May 1978).

Heinkel, R., "A Theory of Capital Structure Relevance Under Imperfect Information," *Journal of Finance* (December 1982).

Higgins, R. and L. Schall, "Corporate Bankruptcy and Conglomerate Merger," *Journal of Finance* (March 1975).

Hirshleifer, J., "The Private and Social Value of Information and the Reward to Inventive Activity," *American Economic Review* (September 1971).

Holmstrom, B., "Equilibrium Long-Term Labor Contracts," Unpublished Working Paper, Northwestern University (January 1981).

Holmstrom, B. R., "Moral Hazard and Observability," *The Bell Journal of Economics* (Spring 1979).

Huberman, G., "The Disciplinary Market: A Multiperiod Agency Problem," Chicago Working Paper (August 1983).

Jen, F. and S. Hamlen, "Net Present Value and Agency Theory in Financial Planning," SUNY/Buffalo Working Paper (January 1984).

Jensen, M. C. and W. H. Meckling, "Theory of the Firm: Managerial Behavior, Agency Costs and Ownership Structure," *Journal of Financial Economics* (October 1976).

John, K. and A. Kalay, "Information Content of Debt Covenants," NYU Working Paper (January 1984).

Kalay, A., "Stockholder-Bondholder Conflict and Dividend Constraints," *Journal of Financial Economics* (July 1982).

Kaplan, R., "The Significance and Investigation of Cost Variances: Survey and Extensions," *Journal of Accounting Research* (Autumn 1975).

Kim, E., W. Lewellen, and J. McConnell, "Financial Leverage Clienteles: Theory and Evidence," *Journal of Financial Economics* (March 1979).

Kim, E., "A Mean-Variance Theory of Optimal Capital Structure and Corporate Debt Capacity," *Journal of Finance* (March 1978).

Klein, B. and K. Leffler, "The Role of Market Forces in Assuring Contractual Performance," *Journal of Political Economy* 89 (August 1981).

Kraus, A. and R. Litzenberger, "A State-Preference Model of Optimal Financial Leverage," *Journal of Finance* (September 1973).

Kraus, A., "The Bond Refunding Decision in an Efficient Market," *Journal of Financial and Quantitative Analysis* (December 1973).

Kreps, D. and R. Wilson, "Reputation and Imperfect Information," *Journal of Economic Theory* 27 (1982).

Lambert, R., "Long-Term Contracts and Moral Hazard," *Journal of Economics* (Autumn 1983).

Lee, W. and H. Barker, "Bankruptcy and the Firm's Optimal Debt Capacity: A Positive Theory of Capital Structure," *Southern Economic Journal* (April 1977).

Leland, H. and D. Pyle, "Informational Asymmetries, Financial Structure, and Financial Intermediation," *Journal of Finance* (May 1977).

Lewis, T. R., "Bonuses and Penalties in Incentive Contracting," *Bell Journal of Economics* (Spring 1980).

Litzenberger, R., "Debt, Taxes and Incompleteness: A Survey," Unpublished Manuscript, Stanford University (1980).

Locke, E. A. and D. M. Schweiger, "Participation in Decision-Making: One More Look," *Research in Organizational Behavior* (1979).

Long, M. and I. Malitz, "Investment Patterns and Financial Leverage," NBER Working Paper (January 1983).

Magee, R. P., "Equilibria in Budget Participation," *Journal of Accounting Research* (Autumn 1980).

Magee, R., "Simulation Analysis of Alternative Cost Variance Models," *Accounting Review* (July 1976).

Mandelker, G. and A. Raviv, "Investment Banking: An Economic Analysis of Optimal Underwriting Contracts," *Journal of Finance* (June 1977).

Marschak, J. and R. Radner, *Economic Theory of Teams*, Cowles Foundation Monograph 22, Yale University Press, New Haven, CT (1972).

Masulis, R., "The Effects of Capital Structure Changes on Security Prices: A Study of Exchange Offers," *Journal of Financial Economics* (June 1980).

Matsumura, E., "Optimal Allocation of Multidimensional Effort in Agency Settings: Theory and Applications," University of Wisconsin Working Paper (March 1983).

McCulloch, J., "The Tax-Adjusted Yield Curve," *Journal of Finance* (June 1975).

Mikkelson, W., "Convertible Calls and Security Returns," *Journal of Financial Economics* (September 1981).

Milgrom, P. and J. Roberts, "Predation, Reputation and Entry Deterrence," Unpublished Working Paper, Northwestern University (June 1980).

Miller, M., "Debt and Taxes," *Journal of Finance* (May 1977).

Miller, M. and K. Rock, "Dividend Policy under Asymmetric Information," University of Chicago, Unpublished Manuscript (1982).

Miller, M. and M. Scholes, "Dividends and Taxes," *Journal of Financial Economics* (March 1978).

Milne, F., "Choice Over Assets Economies: Default Risk and Corporate Leverage," *Journal of Financial Economics* (June 1975).

Mirrlees, J., "The Optimal Structure of Incentives and Authority Within an Organization," *Bell Journal of Economics* (Spring 1976).

Mirrlees, J., "Notes on Welfare Economics, Information, and Uncertainty," in Balch, M., F. McFadden, and S. Wau (eds.), *Essays in Economic Behavior Under Uncertainty*, North-Holland (1974).

Modigliani, F. and M. Miller, "Corporation Income Taxes and the Cost of Capital: A Correction," *American Economic Review* (June 1963).

Modigliani, F. and M. Miller, "The Cost of Capital, Corporation Finance, and Theory of Investment," *American Economic Review* (June 1958).

Modigliani, F. and R. Sutch, "Innovations in Interest Rate Policy," *American Economic Review* (May 1966).

Myers, S., "Interactions of Corporate Financing and Investment Decisions— Implications for Capital Budgeting," *Journal of Finance* (March 1977).

Myers, S., "Determinants of Corporate Borrowing," *Journal of Financial Economics* (November 1977).

Myerson, R., "Mechanisms Designed by an Informed Principal," Unpublished Working Paper, Northwestern University (June 1981).

Myerson, R., "Incentive Compatibility and the Bargaining Problem," *Econometrica* (January 1979).

Orgler, Y. and R. Taggart, "Implications of Corporate Capital Structure Theory for Banking Institutions," *Journal of Money, Credit, and Banking* (May 1983).

Papoulis, A., *Probability, Random Variables and Stochastic Processes*, McGraw-Hill Book Company, New York (1965).

Penman, S., "An Empirical Investigation of the Voluntary Disclosure of Corporate Earnings Forecasts," *Journal of Accounting Research* 18 (Spring 1980).

Pye, G., "The Value of Call Deferment on a Bond: Some Empirical Results," *Journal of Finance* (December 1967).

Radner, R., "Does Decentralization Promote Wasteful Conflict?", Unpublished Working Paper, Bell Laboratories (June 1980).

Raiffa, H., *Decision Analysis*, Reading, Mass.: Addison-Wesley Publishing Co., (1968).

Ramakrishnan, R. and A. Thakor, "Moral Hazard, Agency Costs and Asset Prices in a Competitive Equilibrium," *Journal of Financial and Quantitative Analysis* (November 1982).

Riley, J., "Noncooperative Equilibrium and Market Signalling," *American Economic Review* (May 1979).

Ross, S., "Some Notes on Financial Incentive-Signalling Models," *Journal of Finance* (June 1978).

Ross, S., "The Economic Theory of Agency: The Principal's Problem," *American Economic Review* (May 1973).

Ross, S., "The Determination of Financial Structure: The Incentive-Signalling Approach," *Bell Journal of Economics* (Spring 1977).

Rothschild, M. and J. Stiglitz, "Equilibrium in Competitive Insurance Markets: An Essay on the Economics of Imperfect Information," *Quarterly Journal of Economics* (November 1976).

Rubinstein, M., "Corporate Financial Policy in Segmented Markets," *Journal of Financial and Quantitative Analysis* (December 1973).

Salop, S. and J. Salop, "Self-Selection and Turnover in the Labor Market," *Quarterly Journal of Economics* (November 1976).

Schneller, M., "Taxes and the Optimal Capital Structure of the Firm," *Journal of Finance* (March 1980).

Scott, J., "A Theory of Optimal Capital Structure," *Bell Journal of Economics* (Spring 1976).

Senbet, L. and R. Taggart, "Capital Structure Equilibrium Under Market Imperfections and Incompleteness," *Journal of Finance* (March 1984).

Shapiro, C., "Consumer Information, Product Quality, and Seller Reputation," *Bell Journal of Economics* (Spring 1982).

Shavell, S., "Risk-Sharing and Incentives in the Principal-Agent Relationship," *The Bell Journal of Economics* (Spring 1979).

Smith, C. and J. Warner, "On Financial Contracting: An Anlysis of Bond Covenants," *Journal of Financial Economics* (June 1979).

Solomons, D., *Divisional Performance: Measurement and Control*, New York: R. D. Irwin & Co., (1978).

Sosin, H., "Neutral Recapitalization: Predictions and Tests Concerning Valuation and Welfare," *Journal of Finance* (September 1978).

Spence, M., "Informational Aspects of Market Structure: An Introduction," *Quarterly Journal of Economics* (November 1976).

Spence, M., *Market Signalling: Information Transfer in Hiring and Related Processes*, Harvard University Press, Cambridge, MA (1974).

Spence, M., "Job Market Signalling," *Quarterly Journal of Economics* (August 1973).

Stiglitz, J., "A Re-examination of the Modigliani-Miller Theorem," *American Economic Review* (December 1979).

Stiglitz, J., "On the Irrelevance of Corporate Financial Policy," *American Economic Review* (December 1974).

Stiglitz, J., "Taxation, Corporate Financial Policy and the Cost of Capital," *Journal of Public Economics* (February 1973).

Stiglitz, J. and A. Weiss, "Credit Rationing in Markets with Imperfect Information," *American Economic Review* (June 1981).

Stoughton, N., "Capital Structure Equilibrium When Agents are Asymmetrically Informed," UBC Working Paper (February 1983).

Taggart, R., "Taxes and Corporate Capital Structure in an Incomplete Market," *Journal of Finance* (June 1980).

Talmor, E., "Asymmetric Information, Signaling and Optimal Corporate Financial Decisions," *Journal of Financial and Quantitative Analysis* (November 1981).

Telser, L., "A Theory of Self-Enforcing Agreements," *Journal of Business* (January 1980).

Titman, S., "The Effect of Capital Structure on the Liquidation Policy of a Firm," UCLA Working Paper (1981).

Townsend, R., "Financial Structures as Communication Systems," Carnegie-Mellon University Working Paper (February 1984).

Townsend, R., "Optimal Contracts and Competitive Markets with Costly State Verification," *Journal of Economic Theory* (October 1979).

Trczinka, C., "The Pricing of Tax-exempt Bonds and the Miller Hypothesis," *Journal of Finance* (September 1982).

Warner, J., "Bankruptcy Costs: Some Evidence," *Journal of Finance* (May 1977).

Watts, R. and J. Zimmerman, "Towards a Positive Theory of the Determination of Accounting Standards," *Accounting Review* (January 1978).

Weingartner, H., "Optimal Timing of Bond Refunding," *Management Science* (March 1967).

Weston, J. F., "Developments in Finance Theory," *Financial Management* (Anniversary Issue, 1981).

Williamson, D. E., M. L. Wachter, and J. E. Harris, "Understanding the Employment Relation: The Analysis of Idiosyncratic Exchange," *The Bell Journal of Economics* (Spring 1975).

Zeckhauser, R., "Medical Insurance: A Case Study of the Trade-Off Between Risk Spreading and Appropriate Incentives," *Journal of Economic Theory* (March 1970).

Wilson, R., "The Theory of Syndicates," *Econometrica* (January 1968).

Zimmerman, J., "The Costs and Benefits of Cost Allocation," *Accounting Review* (July 1979).

Subject Index

Certainty-equivalent interest rate, 19, 119, 121, 123
Claimholder payoffs, 16, 143
Coinsurance policy, 128
Coinsurance effect, 130–31
Common stock, 48–50, 74, 98n, 100, 102, 113
  in capital market, 63–66
  risk incentive problem for, 131–32, 134
Complex financial contracts, 2, 4, 80–105, 115, 127
Contingent claim securities, 67–69
Continuous incentive problems, 74–75
Contracts, agent-principal, 4, 26–30, 37, 39, 40, 80
Contracts, enforceable, 26–28, 137
Contractual instruments, agency, 127–30, 140–42
Conversion price, stock, 93–97
Convertible bonds, 19, 75n, 93–95, 97n
Convertible debt, 4, 80, 81, 93–97, 100, 103–5
Convertible securities, 2, 4, 19, 105
Corporate bond pricing, 112–15, 118, 119, 121–23, 125
Corporate by-laws, 4, 80
Corporate debt, 3, 7, 8, 10–11, 18–20, 125
  call provisions in, 4, 86–92
  interest rate of, 5, 19–21, 23, 94, 118–19, 121, 123–26
Corporate finance (theory), 2, 6–24
  with agency problems, 24–40
  without agency problems, reviewed, 2–3, 6–24
Corporate financial management, 2, 6–40
Corporate income, 7, 14
Corporate income tax, 14–18, 20, 24, 58, 121
  agency cost and, 42, 58–60
  firm value and, 7, 18
Corporate tax rate, 112–15
  See also Tax rate differentials; Tax rates

Cost of agency (see Agency—costs; Agency cost function)
Cost of capital, 7, 9n, 17
Cost of debt (see Debt cost; Debt financing)
Cost of equity (see Equity cost)
Covenants, 116, 129n, 136, 140, 141

Debt:
  in capital structure theory, 4–8, 10, 11–13
  and taxes, 14–24
Debt, straight, 4, 103, 107
"Debt and Taxes," 18–21, 24
Debt capital, 3, 41–60, 74–75, 86–88
  equity capital tradeoff with, 42–58
Debt contract, 92–93
Debt costs rationale, agency, 119, 121
Debt costs, agency, 3, 5, 8, 43–60, 114, 119–21, 124, 125
  marginal bankruptcy and, 53–58
  marginal investment incentive and, 51–52
  marginal risk incentive and, 48–51
  tax subsidy and, 15–18, 20, 23, 41–42, 58–60, 114, 117–19
Debt financing, 3, 8, 15–18, 23, 29 31, 35, 38, 85, 91
  and agency debt cost, 119, 121, 122
  See also Agency cost
  optimal capital structure and, 41–60, 65n, 74–75, 124–25
  relative pricing of securities and, 112–26
  tradeoff with equity financing costs, 41–42, 57–58, 74
Debt mechanisms, 3, 7, 10–11
Debt security issue in synergistic risk incentive, 131–34
Debt supply, 7, 121
Debt-to-equity ratio, 20, 21, 42, 45, 60, 65, 74, 116
Debtholders, 34, 63